BASKETBALL BASICS

BASKETBALL BASICS

Drills, Techniques, and Strategies for Coaches

HOWARD MARCUS

CONTEMPORARY
BOOKS

CHICAGO

Marcus, Howard
    Basketball basics : drills, techniques, and strategies / Howard
Marcus.
       p.   cm.
    Includes index.
    ISBN 0-8092-3958-2
    1. Basketball—Coaching.   I. Title.
GV885.3.M27   1991   91-25513
796.332'07'7—dc20   CIP

Published by Contemporary Books, Inc.
Two Prudential Plaza, Chicago, Illinois 60601-6790
Manufactured in the United States of America
International Standard Book Number: 0-8092-3958-2

To all of the players on all of my teams

CONTENTS

Acknowledgments *ix*

Key to Diagrams *xii*

Introduction *1*

1 Why Are You Doing This? *3*

2 Coaching Techniques *7*

3 The Basic Coaching Sequence *13*

4 Footwork on Offense *15*

5 Shooting *23*

6 Rebounding *37*

7 Passing and Screening *45*

8 Dribbling *55*

9 Attacking the Basket *63*

10 Basic Defense *75*

11 Ball-Pressure Defense *87*

12 Offense *97*

13 Transition *107*

14 Breaking the Press *113*

15 Pressing Defense *119*

16 The Season Starts—Tryouts *127*

17 Organizing Practices and Setting Priorities *131*

18 Game-Day Coaching *139*

19 Coaching Junior High and Recreational League Teams   *145*

20 Parents and Children   *149*

21 Conclusion   *153*

    Index   *155*

ACKNOWLEDGMENTS

Thanks to Todd Fitzpatrick for his diagrams and Bill Lovejoy for his photographs.

Thanks to everyone appearing in the photographs: Isaac Bonnaker, Lauren Certo, Alison Erice, Angela Gray, Sophia Howard, Paige Kruger, Jane Macro, Tyrell Zackery McQuitta, Jennifer Poli, Jyoti Raymond, Collin Smith, Jonathan Sylvan, Jennifer Walker, Lilah Walsh, Matt Workman, and Leah Zeazell.

My special appreciation to Freda Sprietsma for her help in preparation of the manuscript.

BASKETBALL BASICS

KEY TO DIAGRAMS

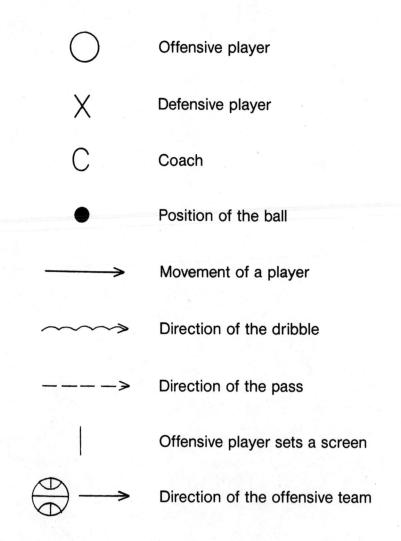

◯   Offensive player

X   Defensive player

C   Coach

●   Position of the ball

⟶   Movement of a player

⟿   Direction of the dribble

⇢   Direction of the pass

| Offensive player sets a screen

⊕⟶   Direction of the offensive team

INTRODUCTION

Picture this scene: the guard passes the ball to the center; the center takes the ball to the basket and scores. The crowd roars as the horn sounds, ending the game. The home team has won on that last-second basket.

When you watch highly accomplished players, basketball looks natural and uncomplicated.

Now look again: the guard is dribbling with his head up so he can see the whole court. He sees that the center is about to get open for a pass. The guard jump-stops in proper balance; he steps to the side and throws a bounce pass that his defender cannot reach. The pass is timed to arrive during that second or two that the center is free of his defender. And the pass is thrown to a spot that cannot be reached by the center's defender.

The center uses a screen set by a teammate to gain a step on his defender. He then cuts sharply to a position along the foul lane just out of the painted area, staying close to the basket but not in the three-second area. He establishes his position with a wide stance, his knees flexed, so that the defender cannot reach around to deflect the ball. The center signals for the ball to be thrown to his right side by stretching out his right hand. Upon catching the ball, he fakes to his right and starts left toward the hoop. He turns 45 de-

grees during his first step, blocking his defender away from the hoop. One dribble is followed by a jump stop at the correct angle to the basket, and the center shoots the ball to complete the play.

Years of coaching and years of practice time made that play successful. To achieve that result, the coach breaks down complex individual skills (such as shooting or driving) into their component parts and teaches each part separately. Then he or she combines the parts. Finally, he blends the skills of each player into an effective team offense and team defense.

That is only part of the job description for a coach. He or she must not only be an effective teacher and a strategist but also be responsible for countless other details such as conditioning, scheduling, tryouts, and transportation. To do the job well, a coach must set attainable goals, be well prepared, and use practice time efficiently.

Basketball Basics is intended to be a complete guide for a coach, parent, physical education instructor, or anyone teaching basketball to beginning- or intermediate-level players. Most beginners are children or teens. Coaching kids does present unique concerns such as a lack of maturity and lack of physical size; the discussions in the book are geared to these concerns. For example, many of my players enter high school with poor shooting techniques—they shove the ball at the basket. This bad habit was acquired during a time when they lacked the strength to reach the basket with their shots; to get extra power, they pushed the ball using the shoulder. Included in the chapter on shooting is a section on recognizing players who are shot-putting the ball and teaching them to use their legs for the necessary power.

My first objective in writing this book was to emphasize the importance of having a clear understanding of what you are trying to accomplish. Do you want to win games, teach fundamentals, prepare a few players to be outstanding, give everyone an equal chance to play, be a role model? The first chapter discusses establishing priorities—many of your choices will depend on those priorities.

Another objective was to focus on effective teaching methods. A coach never has enough practice time; these chapters demonstrate how to convey the material so that players can absorb it quickly and well. Chapter 3 illustrates how to take a new skill from its initial presentation to its advantageous use in a game setting.

My next objective was to provide complete information for teaching individual and team skills. Individual skills are broken down into manageable parts, which are then taught in sequence. Each skill is illustrated by photos and accompanied by one or more drills that isolate the skill so it can be easily taught. The drills are tied into the individual and team skills that follow. For example, the footwork drill is extended into the passing,

shooting, and driving drills; these are combined and expanded into a five-man drill that forms the basis for the offense.

The next chapters present team skills. Specific offenses and defenses are also presented sequentially, with photos and diagrams. I specifically did not select an offense or defense in which players simply repeat a pattern on the court. Rather, I recommend offenses and defenses that require them to concentrate on each new situation and use their fundamental skills. In this way they will acquire a solid foundation of basic skills that will enable them to develop into sound basketball players in the years to come.

The following chapters were designed to present other aspects of coaching: conducting tryouts, organizing practices, and coaching during games.

There are two special chapters: The first is for coaches of recreational league teams; it discusses prioritizing skills to meet the needs of inadequate practice time. The second, for parents who are teaching their children, suggests ways that the parent and child can both have a good time as the child learns the game.

I wrote *Basketball Basics* to suggest an approach to coaching that allows both players and coaches to have a good time. In writing about the complexities of coaching, it is easy to lose sight of the fact that it provides a wonderful opportunity to work with kids who are usually full of energy and joy. Most of all, basketball is fun. I hope this book helps you to be a coach who experiences, and whose players experience, many productive and enjoyable seasons of basketball.

Howard Marcus

1
WHY ARE YOU DOING THIS?

I coach a high school girls' basketball team. As I was starting my first year of coaching, at the junior varsity level, I hadn't given much thought to my purpose, what I would try to achieve. But I was about to.

The varsity coach told me that winning wasn't the most important thing for my team. He wanted the girls who would eventually have a chance to make the varsity team to get a lot of playing time on the JV team and to learn the basic skills necessary to move on to varsity basketball.

About a day later, the school principal called me over and said, "The purpose of coaching is educational. This is a school sport, a school activity, and every school activity has the same basic purpose, which is educational. Winning is nice, but giving the students an appropriate educational experience has to come first."

A few days later, I wasn't too surprised when a teacher friend of mine came to practice, took me aside, and said, "I don't know if you're giving a whole lot of thought to the opportunity you have now that you're coaching. One thing that a coach can do is choose one or two kids a year who are having a hard time and put them on the team. Maybe they're having problems in school or problems at home; they don't have much going right for them. They may be headed for trou-

ble. But they enjoy basketball, and if you give them a lot of support they could really enjoy a positive experience, and that's a start toward giving them meaning and direction in their lives. That can be the most important thing you do as a coach."

After eight years of coaching, each of these thoughts still seems important. I firmly believe that the key to a positive experience for both coach and athlete starts with a clear idea of your purpose and priorities. Whether you're coaching at a school, in a recreation league, or at a camp, I suggest these goals: your team members should learn the positive lessons of sport, learn the fundamentals of basketball, put forth their best efforts, and enjoy themselves.

Attain those objectives and you will be a success. Your players, their parents, school administrators, and you should be well satisfied with a season that has accomplished those goals. And you will be rewarded to see your team members maturing as basketball players and as people through the beneficial influence of participating in your basketball program.

You can expect that your commitment to your objectives will be thoroughly tested. A situation arose not too long ago in which our team was in the last few minutes of a game and the score was very close; my leading scorer, best rebounder, and best defender (all wrapped up in one person) had four fouls. During a time-out, I cautioned her to be careful—one more foul and she would be out of the game.

A few minutes later the whistle blew, and, sure enough, the referee pointed at this player. The other coach called to the ref and said his book showed five fouls. The referee came over and looked at the official score book. It said four fouls—obviously an error.

I knew it was a mistake; the kids on my team knew it was a mistake. If I didn't say anything, my best player would remain in the game.

If winning were the main object, I suppose silence would have been the answer. But if your purpose is educational, instead of looking at this as a disaster you should look at it as an opportunity to stand up and do the right thing. So, with mixed feelings, I said to the referee, "Look, it's five fouls, we agree."

Had I remained silent the message would have been: "It's okay to lie by silence or to win at any cost." But because I spoke up, the message the team got was: "This is what sports are supposed to be about—competing to win but playing by the rules." I wish I had remembered to make that point during our team meeting after the game.

Winning is certainly important to me. I don't want to kid you: I really want our team to win every time out. As a coach, I try to do everything possible to help our team win. Your players want to win too, although most kids handle losing a lot better than their coaches and parents do.

The approach suggested in this book does lead to winning. Your players feel safe knowing that there is a fair set of rules, a coach who respects them as individuals, and teammates who support them. In that climate they learn quickly and the team improves rapidly. Players will give their best effort because they are more confident and not burdened by unnecessary tension and unrealistic

expectations. As a result, they will stay in your program next year. You will find that more players will come out for basketball when they hear that the coach is someone they would want to play for. So this approach sets the stage for your success as a coach.

The key to a successful season lies in how you and your players experience the season, not in your win-loss record. For example, the year before I started coaching, the team's record was 1–17. The players had become accustomed to losing and expected only bad things to happen.

That first season was a long and difficult journey, but our trip from the bottom of the league to respectability was the most satisfying experience I have ever had. We finished with a losing record, 8–9, but by the end of the season we were about as strong as any team in the league. Our turnaround culminated in an overtime win against the first-place team, who had blown us off the court earlier in the season. One of our players, who had never played basketball before that year but had become a very effective rebounder, literally collapsed to the floor when the final buzzer sounded. She was both crying and laughing, exulting over what we had accomplished. None of my teams with winning records in succeeding years have matched that group for team spirit.

Each year, on my team and other teams, I've watched players grow more self-confident and more optimistic; they learn how to win, learn to lose, learn to work hard, learn to work together, and learn to rely on each other. They at times show understanding beyond their years in helping out teammates undergoing crises in their personal lives. I certainly don't attribute all of this solely to basketball or to coaching, but the coach surely plays an important role and can be a positive force by setting the right tone.

There is a dark side to that force: coaches often abuse athletes verbally and emotionally, making them feel that they've failed and eventually turning them off to sports. In a recent study published in a psychological journal, athletes who'd had bad experiences with their coaches repeatedly made comments to this effect: "I was hurt, angry, and frustrated," "I was always unhappy and confused," "It's incredible how long this stayed with me; I felt devastated, I felt insulted." One said, "It's amazing how long people like me carry this experience with them."

Despite the best intentions of the coach, an overemphasis on winning or poor teaching methods can produce this kind of negative experience. On the other hand, when a coach keeps his priorities straight and teaches effectively, both players and coach can have a rewarding, successful season.

And that brings me to another of my goals in coaching: to enjoy the job. I find coaching very enjoyable; in fact, I have always felt that I get at least as much out of coaching as I put into it—and probably more. When I ask myself, Why am I doing this? one of the answers is that it is fun, plain and simple.

2
COACHING TECHNIQUES

REWARD VERSUS PUNISHMENT

There are two well-known coaching methods of motivating players: one is fear of punishment, and the other is praise. This was brought home to me at a clinic for coaches given by Bobby Knight and Mike Krzyzewski ("Coach K"), two of the most successful college basketball coaches in the country.

Picture this: About 200 coaches were sitting in the gym bleachers at San Jose City College. The members of the San Jose City College basketball team, volunteers for the drills Knight and Krzyzewski were going to show us, were seated along the baseline. Knight, who was out by the foul line, said to the team, "Okay, come on out here and let's do some drills." They got up and started to walk toward him. Knight stopped them: "Hold it! Go back and sit down. Look—you probably didn't hear me. What I said was, 'We want to do some drills, and the last one out here is going to do 50 push-ups.' Now come out here, and let's do some drills."

Chairs flew in all directions as the players sprinted toward Knight. Then he said, "Okay, now I want you to get together and tell me who got out here last." The team huddled together and picked the poor guy who was last.

Knight put his arm around him and said,

"C'mon over here—let's go where we can talk privately and no one will hear us." Well, of course, with a microphone on and 200 people in the gym, his words were bouncing around the gym loud and clear. He said to this player, "You know, I've got a pretty bad reputation as being a mean guy and a tough guy, but it isn't true. I'm really a very nice guy, and to show you I'm such a nice guy I'm not going to make you do the 50 push-ups." Knight had been standing a little crouched over, and now he stood up straight and took his arm off the boy. When the young man started walking back to the team, Knight said, "Hold it. I didn't tell you to go anywhere. We're not finished. I'm not going to make you do these 50 push-ups now, but I'm putting them in my pocket, and if you mess up one more time [I'm deleting a lot of expletives here], you're going to do 100 push-ups." Well, for the rest of the day Knight got what he wanted. Everyone was performing, doing exactly what he said and doing it right away.

Coach Knight singled out a player who really did nothing wrong, told that player that he owed the coach something, and threatened him with either embarrassment or punishment to keep him and others motivated and "in line." Coach Knight uses this methodology in dealing with highly motivated young men who are at the highest levels of their sport.

Coach K had another way of relating to the players. In the first five minutes of drilling he learned the names of several of them and gave them praise for what they did. In the first drill he asked the names of two players (William and Ken) and told them to go out and stand at the midcourt line; when the dribbler came upcourt they were to try to steal the ball. When they got into position a few feet from the midcourt line, Coach K immediately stopped the drill and said, "Ken, I want you to repeat my instructions to you." Ken answered, "Stand at the midcourt line and pick up the dribbler." Coach K said, "You're not on the midcourt line, are you? That's where I want you to be." They adjusted their positions. Coach K patted them on the back and said, "Good, William, Ken. Now let's go from here."

Coach Krzyzewski was making sure the drill was done his way, and the players responded to being praised and being acknowledged as people. They carefully followed his directions during the remainder of the drills.

I strongly believe that using praise is the better method for coaching basketball. The combination of praise and instructive criticism sets the stage for a player to learn a skill the way the coach wants it done. On the other hand, telling a player, "You messed up" will often make him feel he is being personally criticized; when a player feels angry or embarrassed, he is not ready to learn. Younger athletes in particular have difficulty putting personal criticism in perspective; they are more apt to feel blamed and become discouraged.

When a player tries something new and gets it partially right, this is a prime teaching opportunity. Rather than making his first comment a critical one, the coach should appreciate what he has just seen: (1) the player has heard what the coach asked him to do, (2) has tried to do what was asked of him, and (3) has partially succeeded.

That is progress! The coach recognizes that progress by praising those aspects that were done correctly. Now the player is ready to hear instructive criticism. At that point the coach tells the player the next step that he needs to take. Instead of saying, "You messed up this part," he says, "Now that you're really learning how to screen properly, the next step is to roll toward the basket after you have set the screen." Right after you have praised the player's accomplishment is the best time to build on that accomplishment.

Here is a fictitious illustration of the advantages of using praise and instructive criticism rather than blame and punishment: Sarah and Mary are fifteen-year-old identical twins who attend different high schools. Each plays on the basketball team, and their basketball skills are identical.

Sarah plays for Coach Down. After practice one day, this is what Coach Down said about Sarah:

"Sarah really screwed up in practice today. We've been practicing three skills in learning to rebound: blocking out the defensive man, taking the rebound at the top of the jump, and turning and throwing a fast outlet pass. Today in the scrimmage Sarah blocked out her man, but not all that well, barely jumped for rebounds, and when she did get a rebound she didn't throw the fast outlet pass.

"I chewed her out good. She gets me angry because she has the ability to do it if she'd only apply herself. There are some kids who are just real hard to coach."

This is what Sarah said about the practice:

"The coach said I really messed up in practice today. I'm trying, but I can't seem to do anything right. I feel like a failure. He told me he didn't know why he ever put me on the team. I dread going out to practice; I may just skip basketball next year."

Coach Up has had his girls practicing the

same skills. This is his evaluation of Mary's progress:

> "When practice started two weeks ago, Mary couldn't block out at all, never jumped for rebounds, and didn't know what an outlet pass was.

> "Today in practice, she blocked out the player she was guarding; it wasn't elegant, but she got the job done. She is starting to jump for rebounds—she never did that before—although her timing isn't good yet. She often waits too long to jump and catches the ball on the way down. I also want her to throw the fast outlet pass; but it takes time to learn these things, and she isn't used to doing them yet. She'll be ready to throw the outlet pass pretty soon now. Mary is doing really well."

This is Mary's view of playing basketball:

> "I had a good practice today. The coach told me I was blocking out much better and that was a solid contribution to the team because we get more rebounds that way, and when we keep the offensive players away from the basket, our team doesn't give up any cheap baskets. The coach showed me how to widen my stance so I could be more effective in blocking out, and I'll be working on that tomorrow. He also said that he saw solid progress in my rebounding because now I'm starting to get off the ground, although I don't have the timing down yet.

> "Today for the first time I thought about looking for the outlet pass, but everything was moving so fast that I thought I'd just keep the ball safe and not try a dangerous pass. Coach keeps telling us to take care of the ball.

> "I'm making real progress, Coach is happy with me, I'm enjoying playing, and I really feel like I'm part of the team effort . . . and this is just my freshman year."

Although their performances in practice were the same, the difference in the girls' perceptions results from the use of praise versus blame as a method of coaching. The player who feels that she is progressing is more apt to take suggestions and to feel confident enough to risk trying new skills.

Coach Up not only told Mary that she'd blocked out her opponent; he said, "This is what you did. You turned toward the basket and then made contact with your opponent. That's good because it takes her a lot longer to get to the basket to try to rebound." And he continued: "If your back is to the basket and you pivot on your inside foot to a wide stance, you can move more quickly to block out the player. With a wider stance, it takes longer still for the player to get around the block. You had a narrow stance, like this, at a point where you should have been in a wider stance, like this." The coach acknowledged Mary's progress and demonstrated the next step toward the desired goal.

Many players find it difficult to drive the ball to the basket. Let's assume that in a scrimmage a player tries for the first time to drive the ball to the basket, but the ball bounces off his foot and out of bounds. The player has attempted what the coach has asked and taken that difficult first step toward the basket; the fact that the ball bounced off his foot is inconsequential to the fact that he has made substantial progress. The coach should stop the practice, compliment the player, and tell him that he'd much rather see him try and bounce the ball off his foot than just shoot from the outside. If the player made a specific mistake in technique, the coach would then correct that error.

With the encouragement of the coach and teammates who are supportive of efforts of this kind, it is a lot easier to take that first step.

KEEP IT SIMPLE

For the most part, your players do not have a lot of experience playing basketball. As with beginners in any endeavor, they are not pre-pared to execute anything complicated. For that reason, it is best to give them a few simple directions that they can apply on the court. For example, the teams we play will often run screens against us. After I show the players what a screen is, my rule is *Never switch on screens.* In other words, the defensive player always stays with the offensive player and must fight his way through or around the screen. Another example relates to shooting. I draw a semicircle about eight feet from the basket and instruct players to always shoot when they have an open shot in that area.

When inexperienced players are on the court they are often confused because they don't know what is happening or why it is happening. Simple rules are intended to offer the players guidelines that apply to a majority of the situations they will face on the court.

It is true that these rules have drawbacks and exceptions, but if you make your directions too complicated, you further confuse the inexperienced player. Keep it simple and your players can get experience while operating under an understandable set of rules. The following season they can learn to switch on screens.

KEEP IT CLEAR

Beginning and intermediate players often are not familiar with basketball terminology. For example, many coaches routinely use terms such as "strong side" or "weak side," "bank shot," "2-1-2," but their players haven't the foggiest idea of what they are talking about. When it's necessary for your team to know what a 2-1-2 is, you'd better put five players on the court in that formation and show them what it means. Then move the players into other configurations and ask team members to name each formation.

Referring to the left or right side of the court can lead to confusion unless you show

players your frame of reference. Have the team stand at midcourt and face one basket. Then explain that left and right are determined from midcourt, facing the basket in question.

I've wasted a lot of time in practice giving lengthy explanations of drills that the players haven't seen before. It's much quicker to simply have them walk through the drill. You can participate as necessary to show them what you want them to do. They'll learn it much faster that way.

TEACH A FEW THINGS WELL

Winning isn't very hard. Just teach a few things well instead of many things poorly.

For example, by the end of the season, my girls' high school JV teams can play solid man-to-man defense (although they don't switch on screens or run complicated pressing defenses); they can rebound properly (but not block out well), and they can move the ball to get a good shot (but not run five-player offensive patterns).

I think the most frequent error made by coaches is trying to teach too many skills. There is simply no way that beginning players are going to learn to pass, dribble, shoot, drive, rebound, screen, block out, play team defense, play team offense, and break the various kinds of full-court presses that they may encounter. The following chapters therefore emphasize the basic skills that can be learned by good athletes in a three-month high school season plus a method of prioritizing these skills to meet more severe time limitations. Chapter 19 prioritizes skills for a junior high school or recreational-league season; Chapter 20 prioritizes skills for parents who are teaching their children.

UNDERSTAND THE PLAYER'S PERSPECTIVE

You may wish that you could win all your games and turn every player into a star; but the kids really don't care much about that. They are not stars, and they know that. They just want to compete and enjoy themselves.

Your players have many other concerns. They want to spend time with their friends, some have jobs, and all have their school work and their families, not to mention the variety of problems that teenagers encounter.

Unfortunately, some of your players are likely to be experiencing some serious personal problems at home, in school, or in their social lives. These problems will affect their interactions with you and with other team members.

A coach's first reaction to a player who is causing problems on the team is to regard the behavior as a challenge to the coach's authority and to read the riot act to the player. Sometimes you need to read the riot act to a player, but it's a good idea to be sure that you fully understand the situation first. Often the behavior is an outgrowth of personal problems rather than a challenge to your authority.

It's a good idea to anticipate situations that will lead to conflicts. For example, every year it seems that at least one practice or game conflicts with a school dance. We try to work around that by rescheduling rather than by putting a kid in a hopeless conflict in which she must choose between the team and a major social event.

MEET PROBLEMS HEAD-ON

Of course, to make matters more complicated, some behavior by the players is a challenge to your authority. For example, if a player doesn't have a legitimate reason for being late or missing practice, this situation needs to be addressed immediately, in a straightforward way.

Make it clear from the first day not only that the players are expected to attend practice but what the consequences will be if they do not. I don't like to take players out of the starting lineup or take away playing time,

but occasionally I will do so. I also consider having the player leave the team for a few days or leave the team altogether if real behavior problems arise.

If you let unacceptable behavior slide, it will undermine the morale of the team. For example, if one of your starters is missing practice but still getting full playing time, your substitutes are probably thinking, "Look, he isn't coming to practice; how come he is getting time and I'm not? It's not fair." This situation erodes your authority as coach and lowers the morale of the team as well.

Without delay, the coach should meet with the player and tell him that he must stop coming late to practice or missing practices. The coach should then lay out the consequences if the problem continues and enforce those consequences in the event the player doesn't conform to the coach's requirements.

The unacceptable behavior can interfere with the progress and morale of the team, and it can ultimately undermine the coach's authority as well. Where a serious personal problem does exist, the coach must carefully weigh the negative effect the player is having on the team against the potential negative impact on the player and the team if the player is dismissed.

COMMUNICATION

Clearly state your expectations of the players. Spell out your rules relating to attending practices, arriving early for games, playing time, etc. When a coach explains his rules or policies to the team in advance, the team has a chance to adjust to those policies and isn't surprised when they are enforced.

At the first team meeting I tell the players specifically what I expect of them. My speech goes something like this:

"I expect you to support your teammates. If a teammate does something well, tell her she did a good job; if a teammate tries something and it doesn't work, acknowledge that she has made a good effort. I don't care whether you like all of your teammates; I don't expect you to. I do expect you to support your teammates. If you have a problem with a teammate, take it up with her directly, and if you can't work it out, bring the problem to me. But don't talk behind a player's back or behind my back, because that just weakens the team.

"I expect you to give your best effort. I don't expect you to make a specific number of points or rebounds, but I do expect you to try your hardest.

"I expect you to come to practices; if you don't, the team is going to suffer. We're going to progress very quickly on a step-by-step basis. If you're not here, you're not going to know what to do. Again, you are going to let your teammates down. If you have to miss practice or a game, ask my permission in advance. If you're too ill to come to practice, let me know through a teammate or have a parent call me.

"Your teammates are here to support you in trying new skills. Even though you may feel nervous or self-conscious at first, take a deep breath and try something new. We all respect that kind of effort.

"Give yourself a break. Don't get down on yourself if you make a mistake. Mistakes happen; even professional basketball players make mistakes."

I also tell the team what they can expect from me. For example, I tell the players that I consider defensive play to be the key to getting playing time. Even players who are not yet able to contribute much offensively can count on some playing time if they are playing solid defense in practice and in games. (Of course, if they are not contributing offensively, their time on the court will certainly be limited.)

One general comment that I always make

to the team is this: "I will never bench you for making a mistake on the court. I will always tell you if I'm upset with you; if I have a problem with you, you're going to hear about it from me. If you don't hear from me, you can assume we're okay." That way, players don't think that they're constantly in the coach's doghouse.

INSIST ON GETTING WHAT YOU WANT

In using praise, I am not suggesting that you settle for less than a player's best effort. At the clinic, both Coach Knight and Coach K kept emphasizing the importance of insisting on excellence and high standards.

Both made the point that players will give you whatever you insist upon. If you settle for sloppy, you'll get sloppy; if you insist that they do it exactly right, they'll do it exactly right. They're looking to you for direction. You're the authority. Praise your players but don't settle for less than their best.

You may find it hard to insist that players keep repeating something until they get it right, but a coach is making a very important point, particularly early in the season, when he keeps insisting that players run a drill properly. There is a clear message to the team that they are going to have to play basketball your way and not expect to get by with a half effort.

Of course, the coach must constantly exercise judgment in determining how much a particular player or, for that matter, the team can accomplish. It is not possible in one year for a coach to take a team of beginners and have them playing at a skill level of a high school varsity team. How far should your team go in one season? As far as the players' best efforts will take you. Depending upon the age of your players, their abilities, and your practice time, you must make a realistic assessment of each player's efforts and the team effort.

3
THE BASIC COACHING SEQUENCE

STEP-BY-STEP— ONE STEP AT A TIME

Picture a guard catching a pass and driving to the basket for a lay-up. Completing that sequence successfully requires each of the following skills: move toward the pass, catch the pass, jump stop, square to the basket, fake the defender, bring the ball close to the body to protect it while taking the first step toward the basket, complete the drive to the basket at a proper angle, and hit the lay-up. Telling a player who doesn't have these skills to drive to the basket is assuring that he will fail.

Likewise, just telling a player to do all of these things is not going to work. Simply understanding what has to be done is not the same as learning the necessary movements and being able to put them in a complete sequence.

The best way I've found to teach skills to players who are not at an advanced level is to teach the skills one step at a time. For example, a guard has to be able to dribble the ball rapidly up the court without looking at the ball. In order to do that, the guard must first be able to dribble the ball, keeping his head up, using proper form, standing in place. Once that is accomplished, he can dribble the ball at a walking pace up the court, then

at a trot, a slow run, and finally at full speed.

When a player learns each aspect properly, he progresses quickly. If he tries to take a shortcut by starting out at full speed, he will progress very slowly. The coach must be certain that there are no gaps in the player's skills. In this case, a player must learn to walk before he can run.

In a game last season, an opposing coach kept urging a player to drive the ball to her left. However, the player could only dribble with her right hand. Our player was over-shifted toward the offensive player's right hand and was able to stop the player cold. The player was in a hopeless predicament: her coach was yelling at her to drive the ball to the left, but she didn't have the necessary skills to do so.

The second part of Step-by-Step is One Step at a Time. Your players will learn much more quickly if they are only asked to learn one thing at a time. Often when it seems that a player ought to be able to learn a skill but is not doing so, that skill is really a combination of skills that needs to be broken down and learned separately. For example, if you tell a beginning player to shoot with the elbow in, follow through, and jump while shooting, it will be nearly impossible to follow all of those instructions. On the other hand, if you have a player shoot against the wall 30 or 40 times with his elbow in the correct position, and do that for two or three days, that first skill will be mastered and he will be ready to move on to the second skill—a proper follow-through.

LEARNING TO USE NEW SKILLS IN A GAME

Let's assume that through your teaching sessions a player now has a reasonable grasp of a particular skill in question—for example, the drop-step move, a basic move for a frontline player. Now it is time for the next step in the sequence: using the move in a scrimmage.

Tell the player prior to the scrimmage that you want him to do the drop-step move at every opportunity. Then adopt special scrimmage rules: Tell the guards to pass the ball to that frontline player very frequently. Instruct the defensive players that when that forward gets the ball they are not permitted to play defense at all against the drop-step move. This gives your player the opportunity to use the skill in a game setting without any opposition.

Watch the progress of the player during the scrimmage and acknowledge that progress when the player uses his new skill. If the players are not doing what you want them to do, stop the scrimmage, again illustrate what you want done, and insist that they use the move in the scrimmage. If you are still not getting results, make the team walk through the move a few times before resuming the scrimmage.

The player should be scoring fairly easily without any opposition from the defense. Of course it's easy to score when there is no

defender; but the point is that the player has now transferred the skill from a drill to a game setting.

After one or two scrimmages, modify the special rules again and tell the defenders to play soft defense. Again, watch the progress of your player to be sure that the player is trying this move in the scrimmage. If he is not, stop the scrimmage and tell the player again what you want to happen. At this point I will often enter a scrimmage in the guard position, tell the point guard to pass the ball to me, and then pass the ball to the forward to be sure that the opportunity for the drop-step move arises.

Once the player has mastered this stage, the defender can play hard defense. Once that has been accomplished—and, again, it should be acknowledged—talk to your player about incorporating this move into the next game. Remember, this is a very important objective for your team because it is the key to inside scoring. I will often tell the team that we'll try this move the first time we get the ball, and I'll repeat this after a time-out. From that point on, your player should be able to incorporate the move into his game.

The basic sequence of teaching a skill is:

1. Isolate that skill and explain it.
2. Isolate that skill in a drill and practice it until it is part of the "muscle memory." Simply telling them isn't sufficient; in the heat of the game, players will only use the moves they have committed to muscle memory.
3. Incorporate the skill into a scrimmage using no defense, then light defense, and then full defense.
4. Finally, incorporate the skill into the game.

4
FOOTWORK ON OFFENSE

Almost all individual skills start with proper footwork. Good footwork will cut down on walking violations, facilitate driving to the basket, improve shooting, and result in fewer intercepted passes. Footwork provides the bridge between beginners' basketball and really learning the game.

In discussing footwork, I will assume that players are right-handed. More often than not, you will have one or two left-handed players on your team. Those players can learn more quickly if they are allowed to maintain their natural preference; otherwise, they are not able to use the skills they have developed and are more likely to be confused. I tell the left-handed players that it is too cumbersome for me to explain everything first for right-handed players and then for left-handed players, that I expect them to use their right foot when I am telling the right-handed players to use their left foot, and so on.

The underlying principle to the material that follows is that players can best learn a simple "always do this" lesson. For that reason, we will always use the left foot, the natural preference for a right-handed player, as the pivot foot. We are not restricting players to moving only to their right, as these drills are intended to teach players to move to both the left and the right. We are simply restricting them to the use of one pivot foot so that they have a clear sense of what to do on the court at all times.

This system of footwork and drills is intended to place the offensive player in proper balance, with an established pivot foot, and in the "triple-threat" position. Figure 4.1 shows a player in the triple-threat position:

Figure 4.1. The triple-threat position: the player can pass, shoot, or drive.

His pivot (left) foot is back, the ball is protected on his left hip, his knees are flexed, and his head is up. His feet are about 12 to 15 inches apart, the front foot about 6 inches ahead of the pivot foot. His feet are in shooting position—he only needs to bring the ball up and square to the hoop. He is also in position to stride forward and pass the ball or to drive to the basket.

FOOTWORK FOR PASSING

Receiving the ball. Assume that the passer is on the player's right as the player faces the basket. With the left foot in place, the player steps toward the ball with her right foot and catches the pass (Figure 4.2). Moving toward the ball when receiving passes is essential—it prevents interceptions. When the player catches the ball, she shifts back into the triple-threat position.

When the ball is coming from the player's left, her left foot remains anchored as the pivot foot; she steps with her right foot toward the ball in front of her left foot. Again, she moves toward the ball to receive it and uses the same pivot foot (Figure 4.3). She catches the pass and returns to the triple-threat position.

Passing the ball. The passer's left foot remains anchored as the pivot foot as she strides forward toward the person she is passing to (Figure 4.4). If the receiver is straight ahead or to the right, the passer steps directly toward the receiver with her right foot when releasing the ball. If the receiver is to the left, again the passer steps directly toward the person with her right foot, but this time the right foot crosses in front of the left foot.

Striding toward the receiver enables the passer to get her weight behind the ball and

Figure 4.2. Receiving a pass from the right: stride forward to meet the ball.

Figure 4.3. Receiving a pass from the left, again using the left foot as the pivot foot.

Figure 4.4. Stride forward when passing the ball.

her momentum in the direction of the pass. It is true that the passer will have to learn head fakes and ball fakes, but these should not be attempted until the basic footwork has been mastered.

PASSING DRILLS

Three players form a triangle about 10 feet apart. Player 1, who has the ball, passes to the player on his right (stepping in that direction with the right foot). The receiving player will step across with his right foot to receive the pass and bring the ball to the triple-threat position. The player then passes the ball to the third player, who repeats the actions of the second player. In this way, the ball goes around the triangle to the right with each player always using the left foot as the pivot, always stepping across with the

right foot to receive the ball, resetting to the triple-threat position, and then striding with the right foot toward the receiver.

It is easy to become confused and try to catch and pass the ball in one motion. Be sure that the player, after catching the ball, resets to the triple-threat position and then goes into his passing motion.

After each player has handled the ball about 20 times, stop the drill and reverse the direction of the ball. Now the first passer is throwing the ball to his left, with the right foot stepping in front of the left. The receiver is stepping to his right with the right foot to receive the ball, bringing the ball to the basic position, and then passing to his left by striding across with the right foot.

This drill is best taught by first working with three players while the others watch; after you're satisfied that each of the three is able to do the drill properly, they can go off to the side and practice 20 repetitions in each direction by themselves. You can then turn your attention to the next three players. This does involve some waiting and watching by the other players the first time you do the drill. After that, it can be made a regular part of the warm-up until you feel all of the players have mastered it.

This drill should also be extended to use six or more players. In this case, three players form the same triangle, with one player or

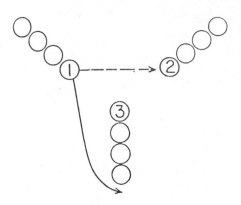

Figure 4.5. Pass-and-cut-away drill.

more waiting behind each of the players in the triangle (Figure 4.5). After player 1 passes the ball to player 2, player 1 runs away from the direction of the pass and goes to the end of the line behind player 3. Player 2 now has the ball and passes to player 3, then player 2 runs in the opposite direction of the pass and gets in the line behind player 1. Player 3 completes the sequence by passing to player 1 and again runs away from the pass and gets in the line behind player 2. The drill is reversed by switching the direction of the ball and the players.

There are four advantages to extending the drill in this fashion. It requires movement on the part of the players after they pass the ball, which is very important on the court.

Figure 4.6. The shooter's stance provides good balance from side to side and front to back.

The players like to do this drill because it can be executed very crisply; this encourages players to equate enjoyment and accomplishment. It is also a good warm-up drill before games. Finally, this drill can lead right into the drill known as "pass and screen away," which is an important component of the offense (Chapter 12).

FOOTWORK FOR SHOOTING

Proper balance is a key to good shooting. Imagine trying to shoot the ball from a moving platform; that may sound absurd, but most players produce that effect because they are moving toward the hoop, away from the hoop, or sideways to the hoop when they shoot. When a player shoots off balance, not only is the shot likely to be inaccurate but it won't give the player any feel for the next shot because the next shot will be completely unlike the first. A player who is in proper balance, on the other hand, is using essentially the same form for every shot.

The triple-threat position provides a solid base for shooting, as there is support from side to side and from front to back (Figure 4.6).

The footwork for shooting is the same as the footwork for passing. To receive the ball from the right, the player steps to the right, receives the pass as before, squares to the triple-threat position, and, without moving either foot again, brings the ball up and shoots.

To receive the ball from the left, the player steps in front and across with his right foot, squares to the basic position, and shoots.

There are several advantages to this footwork:

▶ In the triple-threat position the player is already in proper balance to shoot.
▶ It is uncomplicated and therefore easy to learn.
▶ Because it is simple there is less chance of walking.

▶ The shot can be taken much more quickly, as no additional foot movement is required, giving the defender less time to block the shot.

SHOOTING DRILL

The drill for shooting is very similar to the passing drills; the point guard (player 1) is at the top of the key and the other two players are just outside of the paint, about two feet from the foul line (Figure 4.7). Player 1

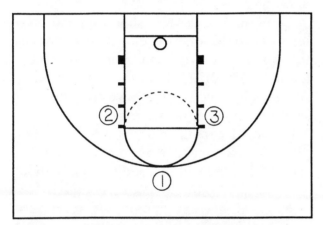

Figure 4.7. Positions for the shooting drill.

passes the ball to the left to player 2. Player 2 catches the ball and returns the pass to player 1. Player 1 then passes the ball to player 3, who squares to the basket and shoots. The footwork is the same as in the passing drill. In this drill, however, player 2 does not pass to player 3, as that pass would not be available on the court during a game.

As player 3 shoots the ball, player 2 moves in to rebound and players 1 and 3 drop back a few steps, ready to play defense. The players reset and repeat the drill until player 3 has taken five shots.

The drill is then run in the opposite direction: player 1 first passes to player 3, who passes back to player 1. Player 1 passes to player 2, who shoots; now player 3 rebounds and players 1 and 2 drop back to play defense.

Finally, the drill is run with player 1 pass-

ing to either player 2 or player 3; this time player 1 steps up to the foul line and shoots when he receives the return pass and players 2 and 3 drop back.

The drill can be extended by rotating the players or bringing in new players.

This drill should be expanded into a five-player offensive drill in a 1-2-2 formation: the point guard is at the top of the circle, the 2 and 3 players (wings) are located at the foul line extended, and the forwards are located about five feet from the paint (Figure 4.8).

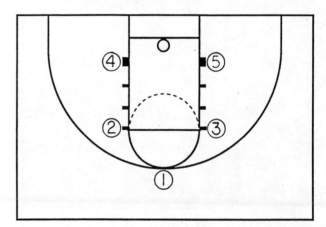

Figure 4.8. Positions for the passing and shooting drill.

When the combination passing and shooting drill is extended to this five-play formation, you have the basis for a 1-2-2 offense with perimeter passing, shooting, and driving. That offense is discussed in Chapter 12.

FOOTWORK FOR DRIVING

The drive to the right starts from the triple-threat position. The player pushes hard off the inside front of the left foot (ball of the foot) and takes a long stride with the right foot past the defender. The long, fast first step is the key to getting by the defender.

The most frequent error committed by players attempting to drive to the basket is to drive too wide around the opposing player. The idea is to beat the defensive player with quickness, but circling too wide

Figure 4.9. Tape on the court helps to show proper footwork for driving.

fashion as the shooting drill. Instead of shooting, the designated player drives the ball to the basket. When the point guard is driving to the basket, player 2 or player 3 sets a screen where the foul line meets the circle (Figure 4.11).

Combination of shooting and driving drill. In this drill, the player has the option of shooting or driving to the basket. The shooting and driving drills are variations of the basic passing drill, so your players are working on their footwork and passing technique in each case.

Combination passing, shooting, and driving drill. In this drill, a designated player has the option of driving, passing, or dribbling the ball. The drill should then be expanded so that all three players have the option of shooting, driving, or passing.

The drill can then be expanded to five players. Now you have an important part of the 1-2-2 offense in place, although without

gives the defender time to catch up. I like to put three pieces of tape on the floor, indicating the position of both feet in the stance of the triple-threat position and the spot where the player's foot should land on the first step of the drive (Figure 4.9).

Driving in the opposite direction also starts from the triple-threat position with the left foot as the pivot foot. The long first step is again made with the right foot off the ball of the left foot, but in driving to the left the right foot steps over and in front of the left foot (Figure 4.10). The player always dribbles with the same hand as the direction in which he is going. The proper techniques for driving are found in Chapter 9.

DRILLS

Driving drill. This drill is run in the same

Figure 4.10. Driving left: the right foot crosses in front of the left (pivot) foot.

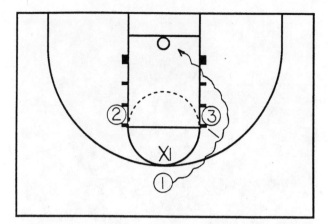

Figure 4.11. The point guard drives to the basket.

any significant player movement. See Chapter 12 for the basic movements of this offense.

No-walk drill. The purpose of this drill is to get players accustomed to starting and stopping the dribble and passing and receiving the ball without walking. Two players start out opposite each other using, for example, the midcourt circle (Figure 4.12). The player with the ball starts to dribble to the right, pushing off with the left foot. The dribble commences before the left foot leaves the ground. The player takes two dribbles,

Figure 4.12. Starting the no-walk drill.

following the circle approximately halfway around, and comes to a jump stop facing across the circle. The player with the ball has now taken the position initially held by the other player. As soon as the player with the ball has started dribbling, the other player fakes to the left and cuts to the right, following the circle halfway around, comes to a stop, and prepares to receive the ball.

Then the player with the ball, using the left foot as a pivot foot, passes the ball to the other player. The other player uses the left foot as a pivot foot and strides forward with the right foot to meet the ball. The player resets, and the drill continues in the same fashion.

After each player has handled the ball about eight times, the players reverse direction. In running the drill to the left, the left foot is still used as the pivot foot. Dribbling is done exclusively with the left hand, and the first step of the dribbler is with the right foot stepping over and in front of the left foot.

CUTTING

Cutting means moving without the ball to get into an open position to receive a pass, set a screen, or rebound.

Players don't automatically make the connection between executing a good cutting move and getting open to receive the pass. Instead, they tend to either stay in place or jog to an open area of the court. This gives the defender a much greater opportunity to steal the ball; even if the pass is completed, the defender has ample time to guard the offensive player who receives the pass. On the other hand, players who are able to execute the cut move properly are able to get open to catch the pass and have an extra step on the defender in making an offensive move.

Whether a player is standing still or running, the cut is accomplished by planting the

Figure 4.13. Cutting to get open: push hard off the ball of the foot.

Figure 4.14. A light, two-foot landing completes the jump stop.

outside foot (the foot opposite the direction of the cut) and then pushing hard off the ball of that foot (Figure 4.13). The cut is usually accompanied by a fake (see Chapter 7).

JUMP STOP

Most beginning players don't appreciate the value of the jump stop; its importance must be emphasized.

The jump stop is used to terminate a dribble without walking and to receive a pass in such a way that either foot can be used as the pivot foot.

To execute the jump stop, the dribbler takes one soft, short step with the left foot and then jumps softly off the left foot to a landing with both feet hitting the floor at the same time (Figure 4.14). The player should be in proper balance, not falling forward. This is the correct way to stop the dribble.

A lot of walking violations occur because the player is off balance when he stops while pushing the ball down the court and then drags his pivot foot as he falls forward. The

jump stop puts him in balance so that he does not drag the pivot foot. It also puts the player in position to pass the ball quickly and perhaps begin a cut to the basket. The jump stop also leaves the dribbler in proper balance to shoot.

Jump-stop drills. The jump stop is first drilled without the ball. Players line up on the baseline, comfortably spaced, and start down the court at a slow jog. When you call "stop," they come to a jump stop; when you call "go," they start again. When they have learned the proper movement going slowly and without the ball, first speed up the drill so they can come to a jump stop at high speed. Then slow the drill down again and repeat the process with each player dribbling a basketball.

The same technique is employed to receive a pass. While the ball is in the air, the player who is going to receive the pass executes the same jump-stop move. The player catches the ball in the air and lands with both feet on the ground at the same time.

5
SHOOTING

RECOGNIZING BAD HABITS

The sections that follow are an attempt to develop an effective, simple shooting stroke—one that can be easily repeated and therefore is more reliable at the outset, and particularly more reliable when the player is tired at the end of a game.

The shooting machine that we are trying to build is always in balance, has a minimum number of moving parts, and is set up square to the basket.

Most players have several poor shooting habits: pushing the ball, being out of balance, holding the ball incorrectly, shooting the ball on too low a trajectory. Each of these habits, if not corrected, will lower a player's shooting percentage.

Most kids have had at least some experience shooting a basketball while growing up. The problem is that they were shooting a ball that was too large and too heavy at a basket that was too high to reach with a good shooting motion.

The result is that most beginning basketball players have learned to "push" the ball—to move the right shoulder (for right-handed shooters) forward as they shoot. When the shoulder moves forward during a shot, there is an almost complete loss of touch. It's like trying to open a combination lock with your shoulder muscles instead of your fingertips. A player who shoots with the shoulder moving forward will not produce a consistent shot or one that can stand up to the pressure of a game.

Another way of getting extra energy into a shot is to twist the wrist just as the ball is released, which puts a whiplike action on the shot. Unfortunately, while this does help the ball reach the basket, like the push, it assures that very few shots will actually go in.

It's easy to spot a player who twists his wrist when he shoots: have the player hold the basketball so that the seam that runs around the ball is parallel to the floor (Figure 5.1). When the player shoots the ball properly, the wrist follows a straight path and continues toward the basket. The seam holds its position parallel to the floor as it spins.

If the wrist twists from right to left, for example, the ball will acquire sidespin in the same direction (Figure 5.2), and the seam will no longer be parallel to the floor. The coach can most easily spot this problem by standing directly behind the player as he shoots.

Most beginning players are moving toward the basket or at an angle to the basket when they release their shots. Players who are moving when they shoot the ball are taking a different shot each time. It is far more difficult for the brain to calculate the correct distance for the shot and transmit that infor-

Figure 5.1. Shooting with the seam parallel to the floor enables the shooter to see if his hand is twisting upon releasing the ball.

Figure 5.2. The shooter's hand twists from right to left, which puts sidespin on the ball.

mation to the "touch" of the shooter. See how many shots you can make from 10 feet while running toward the basket compared with shots that you make when you are stopped.

Players shooting from a balanced position with a minimum of moving parts and aligned as much as possible on a straight line to the basket are able to repeat the shot so that it becomes a routine, mechanical act that can be repeated with a greater degree of accuracy.

Most players will find altering their shooting style to be the most difficult change to accept. They will tell you that it feels weird or awkward to be shooting in the style that you suggest.

Your players may assume that what "feels right" to them is right. I like to explain to players that what they're doing feels right to

them only because they are used to doing it—it is a habit and it feels comfortable. You must insist that they adapt to the shooting style you require.

BODY POSITION

The stance for the triple-threat position provides the proper balance for shooting. With both feet spread apart somewhat, the shooter has stability from side to side. With one foot ahead of the other, the shooter is also in a position not to sway forward. As shown in Figure 4.6, the knees are bent comfortably, the back is straight, and the head is erect. The shooter's weight is equally distributed from side to side and back to front to prevent any swaying motion.

The shoulders and hips are square to the basket: a straight line through the hips and through the shoulders would be perpendicular to a straight line to the basket. If the hips or shoulders are twisting when the shot is taken, the body is rotating, which makes the shot more difficult.

Note that the right forearm is virtually straight up and down; this results from the elbow being in rather than flying out to the side (see Figure 4.6). Figure 5.3 shows the elbow in *incorrect* position: this puts sidespin on the ball, which often causes shots that hit the rim and backboard to spin away; it also interferes with the direction of the shot, as one part of the body is now out of the straight line to the basket and is less stable.

Figure 5.4. The ball is well behind the elbow before the jump shot is released.

Only Two Moving Parts

When the basketball is shot properly, two joints of the upper body do the basic work: the elbow and the wrist. In Figure 5.4, the shooter's arm is bent at the elbow and the ball is much closer to her body than her elbow is. By shooting the ball from above her head, she is able to start in a position that gives the lower arm a significant range of motion.

In Figure 5.5, the shooter's forearm is straight up and down and is in a weaker position. The difference is this: in moving her forearm toward the basket she is able to generate a significant amount of power as her arm moves forward before it reaches the position shown in Figure 5.5. This extra power enables the shooter to increase her shooting range significantly. It also makes the shot harder to block because the defender has to reach farther.

Figure 5.3. Incorrect shooting position: the right elbow is flying out.

Figure 5.5. The shooter loses power by not bending the elbow farther back.

The wrist is also cocked back just before the shot is released. This enables the hand to impart power to the ball as it moves toward the basket. The wrist should be bent until wrinkles show on the back of the hand and no farther (Figure 5.6). Using the elbow and wrist correctly to shoot the ball increases a player's shooting range by a few feet.

The key to teaching shooting effectively is to require players to stay within their effective shooting range until they have learned the basic motion. Keep them within six feet of the hoop; as soon as players start moving farther than their comfortable shooting range allows, they usually start to push the ball with the shoulder or twist it with the wrist to get the extra distance. The extra distance for longer shots must come from the legs and not the upper body (long-distance shooting styles are discussed later in the chapter).

Figure 5.6. When holding the ball to shoot, bend the wrist back until it wrinkles.

Figure 5.7. The fingers of the hand are spread out on the ball.

The Position of the Hands

All five fingers of the shooter's hand are spread out on the ball, as shown in Figure 5.7. The palm is not in contact with the ball: the shaded area in Figure 5.8 touches the ball; the unshaded area does not.

Letting the ball rest on the palm of the hand is a common error. This gives the shooter a little extra power but produces shots that have no spin and little touch. Another common error is supporting the ball entirely with the fingertips. This takes away almost all of the power of the shot.

The position of the left hand should be mostly on the lower half of the ball, with the palm almost facing the shooter (Figure 5.9). When a player raises her left hand above the seam and moves it toward her face, the hand tends to stay on the ball during the shot and push it off line. Figure 5.10 shows a player

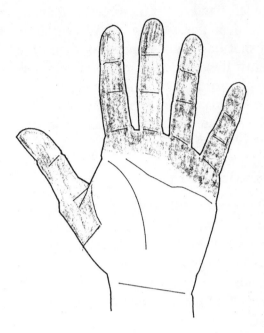

Figure 5.8. The shaded areas of the shooter's hand are in contact with the ball as he prepares to shoot.

Figure 5.9. The ball is held just off the palm.

Figure 5.10. Holding the ball incorrectly: the left hand throws the shot out of balance.

with the left hand in the incorrect position: it is taking over the shot by changing a one-handed shot into a two-handed shot with the ball being handled in a lopsided manner. The purpose of the left hand is only to hold the ball steady as it is being raised into shooting position. The left hand is entirely off the ball when the ball is shot.

The Position of the Ball

For a jump shot, the ball is held above the forehead on a line above the nose (see Figure 5.4). For a one- or two-handed set shot, the ball is held at or above chest height and at the midline of the body (Figure 5.11). The alignment is important because the shooter

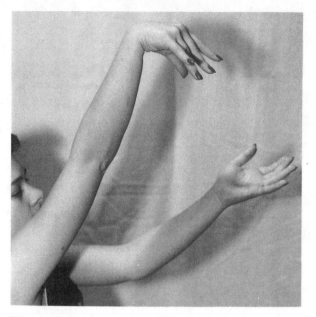

Figure 5.12. A limp wrist is the sign of a good follow-through.

looks at the basket essentially from the midline of her body; if she is shooting the ball from the side, such as from off the shoulder, she is not seeing the line that the ball will travel to the basket.

When the ball is released, the lower arm and hand move directly toward the basket, with the hand following through toward the basket and ending up on line with the basket in a limp position (Figure 5.12). This motion imparts backspin to the ball and allows the player to develop a soft touch: the backspin slows the ball when it hits the rim, so it is more likely to bounce in than a shot with no spin or overspin. It also makes the bounce more upward than forward, which again increases the number of baskets made, as the ball will more often bounce back into the basket. The player should concentrate on the touch of the shot by trying to feel the ball leaving the fingertips.

The shooter's eyes should be fixed on the basket (when using the backboard on the shot, the player should pick out the target on the backboard). This helps to keep your head still during the shot and also improves concentration.

Figure 5.11. Body position for a one-handed set shot.

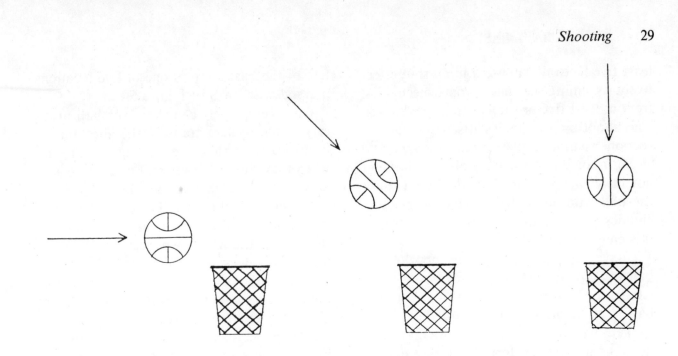

Figure 5.13. Shooting the ball higher gives the shooter a greater margin for error.

Shoot the Ball High

Almost all young players shoot the ball too low. A high-arc shot opens up the basket more.

As illustrated in Figure 5.13, there is no way a ball traveling parallel to the floor can go in the basket. As the angle of the shot increases, there is more room for error. Clearly, the greatest chance for the ball to go in is when it is coming straight down.

Incidentally, this is why a ball shot off the backboard, with proper backspin, is so effective. When the ball hits the backboard with backspin, it comes down at a more severe angle than a shot without spin. With that angle, it is as close as possible to coming straight down into the hoop. For this reason, I like to have my players shoot the ball off the backboard whenever they're at a 45-degree angle to the basket (Figure 5.14).

The proper height for a shot varies with the distance of the shot and the height of the player. One way to gauge the proper height is to have the player shoot a baseline jump shot. By standing 90 degrees to the line of the shot, you can measure the high point of

the shot by visually marking where it passes against the backboard. On a 10-foot shot, the top of the ball should nearly reach the top of the backboard, which is 13 feet above the floor.

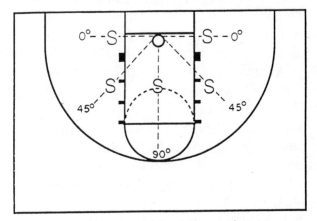

Figure 5.14. Shooting and driving angles.

SHORTER-DISTANCE SHOTS

The coach must first determine whether the player is tall enough or strong enough to shoot a jump shot. Most players who are at least five feet tall can use a jump shot effectively, assuming they have proper mechanics, from at least five or six feet from the basket. The shooting mechanics discussed in this section assume a player has the size and strength for a jump shot. A player who does not have that size or strength should shoot the ball from chest height (the proper mechanics for these shots are discussed later in this chapter).

I have the players begin by shooting the ball off the wall, standing just about three feet from the wall, or I have them shoot the ball straight off the backboard, not at the basket. The idea is to concentrate on repetitions using proper form, not on making baskets. The whole team can do this at the same time.

Players next stand about two or three feet from the basket at a 45-degree angle. From this distance, they can easily reach the basket using only their elbows and wrists. I have them work on getting the ball in the proper position above their heads and holding the ball properly, following through properly, and keeping their elbows in. Those changes are inserted one at a time until each is mastered. Players very quickly learn to shoot these easy shots with some consistency.

As soon as players are able to make five or six in a row, I ask them to try to "feel" the shot—to be aware that they are using the same motion each time and to try to get the shooting motion to be a more mechanical one. After they have taken two or three shots, I have them close their eyes and keep shooting. Most players can make point-blank shots fairly easily, at least one or two of them, with their eyes closed. I tell them that they were able to make those shots with their eyes closed because they were shooting the ball with better form and touch. This increases their confidence in the difficult transition to good mechanics.

After the players have achieved the proper form, I restrict their shooting to within a few

feet of the basket, from one of five locations marked with an S in Figure 5.14.

Once the players can shoot the ball properly, I have them transfer the shot into a jump shot, so they are leaving the ground when they shoot. We are still taking the shot only from right next to the basket.

Players should release the ball at the top of their jump. I illustrate this by first shooting the ball on the way down, then shooting the ball on the way up, and then shooting the ball at the top of the jump. Some players like to shoot the ball on the way up, and I don't object to that, as it is useful for getting greater power as they move farther from the basket later on (although there is some loss of touch).

Once they can shoot the ball properly, the players then take jump shots, using proper form, from different spots on the court that are within five feet of the basket. Shots taken from 45 degrees are shot off the backboard, and all other shots are straight in.

The next step is to pass the ball to a player who moves at random around the area within five or six feet of the basket taking jump shots. The coach passes the ball 10 times to the player, who is moving between each shot. The player should receive the ball with the proper footwork, square to the basket in the triple-threat position, and shoot the ball with proper form. The player can begin by walking from spot to spot and then move progressively more quickly from place to place as he becomes more proficient.

After players are able to handle this drill smoothly, two players can take turns making 10 feeding passes and taking 10 shots. At this point, they should be using the skills in a scrimmage and be ready to shoot the ball from this distance in competition.

Your players have now achieved most of their goals as shooters in that they are able to convert their best scoring opportunities into baskets a reasonable percentage of the time.

ROUTINE

In order for your team to win, your shooters have to be able to put the ball through the basket with some consistency. That requires a shooting motion that is both sound and can be repeated with every shot.

I want players to have the objective of taking the same shot every time. As soon as a player begins hitting the short jump shot, I say, "Think of this as your shot; you want to take this shot every single time. You're square to the basket, you're jumping straight up, you're feeling the ball leave your fingertips with your eyes on the basket. This is the 'Jennifer' shot."

A player who is able to shoot with the same body position and with the same mechanics time after time can become a touch shooter because that player establishes the feel of the shot and can repeat the shot or make adjustments as necessary. The player who is shooting from a different position each time has no hope of making corrections because the upcoming shot is so much different from the one that preceded it.

Watching college or professional players shoot foul shots is a good way to appreciate the importance of establishing a routine. They usually bounce the ball once or twice, take a deep breath, and shoot the ball. The purpose of the deep breath is to have the body as still as possible during the shot. Establishing this routine helps them repeat the same shot, particularly under the pressure of shooting when the game is on the line. Work with your players to have each establish a specific routine that involves bouncing the ball a fixed number of times and taking a deep breath before shooting.

The players should also establish a routine for taking all of their other shots. Basically, they should be aware of being set in the shooting position, of jumping, and of following through toward the basket (or feeling the ball leave the fingertips). Taking the same shot in the same way each time, adjusting only for distance, is absolutely essential in shooting from any place on the court.

The importance of being in proper position and set to shoot before taking the shot cannot be overstated. Most inexperienced players rush their shots because they consider it to be humiliating to have a shot blocked. I would rather have my players shoot 100 percent of their shots without rushing, even if that means that 20 percent or 30 percent are blocked. When a player rushes shots, even if none are blocked the chances are very great that all or almost all of the shots miss.

MEDIUM- AND LONG-DISTANCE SHOTS

Each player has a different effective shooting range, depending upon size and strength. As players move farther from the basket, they can continue to use the jump shot by bending more at the knees and getting more upward spring into the shot. But as they reach the outer limits of their jump-shooting range, they will often start to push the ball again to get extra distance. The coach should review the limits of each player's effective shooting range. If they are using their legs to get spring and still cannot reach the basket comfortably, they have exceeded their shooting range. Players should know their distance limit for shooting the jump shot in a game.

Shooting from a longer distance—out near the foul line—requires a different shooting style, although most of the principles remain the same. The shot is taken from the same shooting position, only this time it is launched from chest height rather than from the height of the player's forehead.

The ball can be shot with one or two hands. The coach and the player should determine which style seems more effective. The difficulty that players often encounter in using the two-handed shot is a lack of symmetry: players tend to hold the ball with their dominant hand in a stronger position and push the ball more with their dominant arm.

Figure 5.15. Holding the ball for a two-handed set shot.

ing with proper mechanics. But the successful three-point shot does offer an important opportunity: it somewhat demoralizes the other team, particularly at the elementary levels of basketball. If you are only scoring about 15 to 30 points a game, one three-point shot represents 10 percent to 20 percent of your offense.

Before I allow players to take three-point shots in the game, I have them take ten shots in practice. Players who miss everything more than once are not allowed to take the shot in the game. Players who are able to hit 3 out of 10 in practice and not miss everything more than once are allowed to take the shot from one particular place on the court where they feel most comfortable, usually from the top of the key.

The ball should be held as shown in Figure 5.15 for the two-handed shot. The same areas of the hands touch the ball as in the one-handed shot. Otherwise, the mechanics for the two-hander and the one-hander are the same.

In order to get additional leverage into the shot, the player should bend her knees more, with the rear end going back and down somewhat (Figure 5.16). The player should then spring straight up, not toward the basket, as the ball is shot. This method dramatically increases a player's shooting range, although as the distance from the basket increases, accuracy will diminish.

Taking three-point shots is a waste of time if players cannot reach the basket by shoot-

Figure 5.16. Springing upward from a crouched position provides power for the shot.

RUNNING LAY-UPS

Ideally, players should approach the basket for a running lay-up from a 45-degree angle (see Figure 5.14) and use the backboard. If an approach from 45 degrees is not possible—on a drive from the baseline or down the center of the court, for example—players should put the ball directly into the basket and not use the backboard.

One of the main reasons for missed lay-ups is approaching the basket at the wrong angle and then trying to use the backboard. For example, a player coming in at too shallow an angle (too close to the backboard) often has his shot bounce along the back of the rim and roll off the other side. Players approaching from, say, 60 degrees get too close to the basket and shoot the ball from underneath the rim. The ball usually rolls off the near side of the rim.

You should emphasize the proper angle in your running drills. For example, have two players pass the ball back and forth while running downcourt about 10 feet inside the side boundaries. When they reach an angle of 45 degrees to the basket, they should cut directly for the hoop (Figure 5.17).

The other common problem is shooting the ball too hard off the backboard. There are two ways to soften the shot. In practicing breakaway lay-ups, players should slow down during the last two or three steps to the basket. This will enable them to bring the ball under control. Breakaway lay-ups should be practiced first with no defense and then with a defender two or three steps behind.

I recommend teaching players to shoot the ball underhanded in order to soften their shots, except that most players under five feet tall are better off shooting the ball in the overhand style. On an ordinary shot, the ball is essentially motionless and the player has to supply the force to the shot. On a breakaway lay-up, the ball is already traveling fast

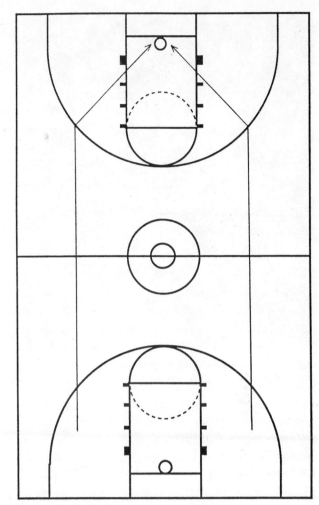

Figure 5.17. Full-court lay-up drill.

enough and does not need any additional force to reach the basket. The standard overhand shot involves arm movement forward that puts more speed on the ball. The underhand shot provides a softer touch: the player needs only to lift the ball into the air, and the ball's forward momentum will carry it to the basket.

In shooting the ball underhanded, the right hand is directly below the ball and the left hand is on the top of the ball somewhat to the left (Figure 5.18); the left hand releases just before the ball is flipped in the air. The ball is held with the arm fully extended and angled up toward the hoop (Figure 5.19). The ball should be released by a flick of the wrist just a foot or two from the

Figure 5.18. The left hand is somewhat on top of the ball at the start of the underhand lay-up.

basket at the top of the player's jump.

The right-handed player approaching from the right side of the basket shoots the ball jumping off the left foot using the right hand (Figure 5.19). Some players feel more comfortable going off the right foot; these players are going to make an unacceptably low percentage of their lay-ups because they will be out of balance when they release the shot. A player shooting a lay-up should be in a position similar to that of a hurdler, with the left leg forward and the right leg back, the right arm forward and the left arm back. This places the player in proper balance.

To stop players from shooting off the wrong foot, have them stand with feet together, at a 45-degree angle and two steps from the basket. They take one step with the left foot and shoot the ball with the right hand. This shot must be taken overhand because an underhand shot can only be practiced at full speed. The players repeat this motion twenty times. At the next practice, have them stand three steps from the basket. Now they first step with the right foot and

Figure 5.19. The right arm is fully extended and angled upward in shooting the underhand lay-up.

then with the left and shoot. Again have them do twenty repetitions.

The drill is repeated from one step farther from the basket each day until players are starting at about 15 feet from the basket and taking the shot on the run. Next, they can start shooting the ball underhanded; finally dribbling can be added. This skill can be learned over a period of two to three weeks.

I prefer to teach my players to shoot from the left side as well; the shot is taken with the left hand off the right foot. I do make exceptions, however, and allow some players to shoot the ball with the right hand. I do this as a practical matter because some players will be in a breakaway position two and three times a game from the left side and be unable to make any of the lay-ups. These are too many baskets to lose while a player is learning.

Another way to shoot a lay-up on a fast break is to jump stop (see Chapter 4) two or three feet from the basket and bank in a jump shot. This technique is often useful for any players who have persistent trouble making breakaway lay-ups. Defensive players usually cannot stop and react quickly enough to block the shot.

6
REBOUNDING

BE AGGRESSIVE

At higher levels of basketball, successful rebounding depends on having tall players who can block out their opponents and jump high to control the backboards. At the beginning levels of basketball, other factors are more important. The key to successful rebounding at the elementary levels of basketball is to train your players to move quickly to the correct area of the court and to go after the ball aggressively.

Most beginners will either watch a shot and not move to rebound the ball or watch a shot, wait for it to hit the rim, see which direction it is going, and then start moving toward the ball. Also, many players are not prepared to fight for rebounds when they are just learning the sport. Most of the girls on my teams are somewhat timid on the court at first. However, after some drills designed to emphasize aggressiveness and rebounding skills, they rapidly become more aggressive.

I start off this process by giving them a speech that goes something like this: "I don't want you to be shy; I don't want you to be sweet; I don't want you to be gentle out on the court. I want you to be aggressive, be tough, and play hard.

"I am not talking about injuring the other players, but I am talking about being determined to dominate the other players offensively and defensively. If our team has the ball, it's ours, and the other team can't have it. Period. If there is a loose ball, we'll dive for it, and we'll get there first because we want it more. Loose balls are ours, period. If the other team has the ball, it's also ours. We loaned it to them for a while, and now they won't give it back, so we're going to have to take it back."

Then I show them a picture of Lorenzo Charles, a member of the North Carolina State team that won the NCAA Championship in 1983. Charles had just pulled down a rebound and is protecting the ball and baring his teeth at the opposition. His message is very clear: "This ball is mine, and that's the end of the discussion."

One year we built an armlike device that extended from the wall and held a basketball suspended by an elastic band. The height of the ball could be adjusted for players working on jumping for rebounds. After my speech on being aggressive, the first girl to try the device pulled the ball down so hard that she ripped the arm right off the wall. Practice stopped at that point in order to present the first Aggressive Player of the Day award.

AGGRESSIVENESS DRILLS

I use two drills for encouraging aggressive play, although I don't use them too often or for too long out of concern for the players' safety. One is called "Dog Fight." Players form three lines—one where the foul line meets the circle at the left side, one on the foul line, and one where the foul line meets the circle at the right side (Figure 6.1).

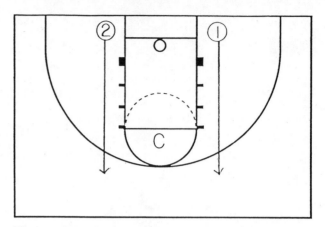

Figure 6.2. Aggressiveness drills: "Scramble" (fighting for the ball and taking it to the hoop).

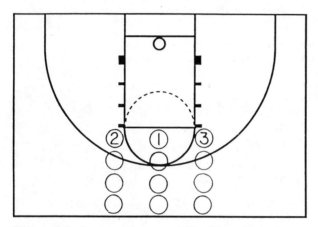

Figure 6.1. Aggressiveness drills: "Dog Fight."

Player 1, on the foul line, shoots; if she misses, players 2 and 3 try to get possession of the ball and play one-on-one until one of them makes a basket. The player can pass to the coach and get a pass back, and no one is concerned with walks, fouls, or out-of-bounds calls. The player who makes the basket stays in the drill and goes to the end of the foul-shooting line. The defensive player who gives up the basket is out. The foul shooter goes to one of the other lines. If the foul shooter makes three in a row, the other two players are out.

The other drill, called "Scramble," starts with players in two lines out-of-bounds, one on either side of the basket, ready to run the length of the court (Figure 6.2). The coach (C) stands at the near foul line with a rack of basketballs. As the players run past him, he can throw the ball down the court, hand it to either player, roll it, throw it up in the air, off

a wall, and so on. The object of the drill is to gain control of the ball and take it the length of the court to score.

MOVE TO THE BASKET AS SOON AS THE SHOT IS TAKEN

Unless they learn to do otherwise, players generally watch a shot until about the time that it hits the basket; then they start moving for the rebound. I illustrate this problem by having someone shoot the ball from just beyond the foul line, and I station myself about eight feet from the basket between the shooter and the basket. I tell the team that this is how not to rebound. I face the shooter, and as the shot leaves her hands, I say, "Oh, look, there goes a shot. Now it's hitting the basket. I ought to go over and get that rebound." Meanwhile, my eyes follow the ball as it passes over my head and goes to the basket. I point out where I am standing when the ball hits the basket.

I then demonstrate the correct way to turn and run to the basket as soon as the shot is taken so the team can see the difference in my position when the ball hits the basket.

Drill. The drill for learning this skill is essentially the same as my demonstration: two lines of defensive rebounders head for the basket as soon as the shot is taken. I do the shooting from a rack of balls. One of the two rebounders must get the ball and return it to the rack. The rotation goes from the front of one line to the back of the other line. I always have my guards participate in these drills as well because I expect them to be active defensive rebounders.

FIND A GOOD REBOUNDING POSITION

The most efficient places to rebound are noted in order of preference in Figure 6.3. The two places marked with the number 1 are the best locations for most rebounds. Of course, the best location also depends upon the spot where the shot is taken. For example, if the shooter is on the left side of the court, the best spot is position 1 on the right side of the court. Usually, there isn't sufficient time for a rebounder to switch sides of the court, so a simple, consistent instruction would be to run to position 1 on the side of the court that you are on.

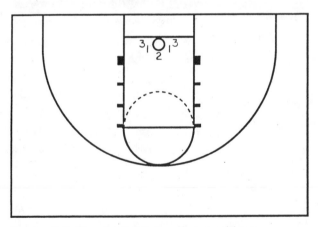

Figure 6.3. The best rebounding positions.

Position 2 is the second-best location. For shots taken from the center of the court, it is probably the best location. Position 3 is usually available to rebounders arriving late after the good positions have been taken, but it is a lot better than not being next to the basket at all. Sometimes your players may take a poor position, directly behind an op-

ponent, rather than an open spot. One of the most frequently called fouls is "over the back." The referees are always watching the rebounders, and trying to reach over the back of an opponent for the ball usually draws a foul.

If the prime rebounding spots are not available, players should just go somewhere around the basket. Especially among beginners, there are plenty of long rebounds that go over the heads of the players who are in the prime areas. This is even more true with the three-point shot: Three-pointers tend to go in, miss everything, or carom out a good distance from the basket. Having four or all five of your players responsible for defensive rebounding can be particularly rewarding at the beginning levels of play.

REBOUNDING DRILLS

The first drill for learning this skill is essentially the same as the drill for moving to the basket as soon as the shot is taken. It can be made more difficult by having two offensive rebounders trying to get the ball as well. The position of the players on the court when the shot is taken would then be as shown in Figure 6.4; you would then have four lines of players and the rotation would be from line 1 to line 2 to line 3 to line 4, etc.

The next drill would be to have all of the

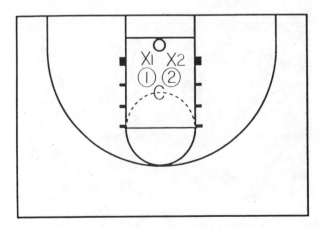

Figure 6.4. Two-on-two rebounding drill.

players on the court, with the offensive team taking the perimeter shots and all of the defensive players practicing going for the rebounds. Have two or three offensive players going for the rebounds too.

The next step is to emphasize aggressive rebounding in your scrimmages. Focus on the rebounding aspect of the scrimmage, and stop the action when necessary if particular players are not going hard for the rebounds.

JUMP WITH ARMS EXTENDED

Many inexperienced players don't jump for rebounds. They wait for the ball to float to earth before reaching for it. You want to be sure that players are catching rebounds at the top of their jump.

The player in Figure 6.5 is catching the

Figure 6.6. Fully extended arms get the greatest height in rebounding the ball.

Figure 6.5. The rebounder catches the ball a foot lower because her arms are bent at the elbows.

ball with her arms bent at the elbow at almost a 90-degree angle. This is the way the majority of players catch rebounds if they are not coached to do otherwise. The arms should be fully extended as shown in Figure 6.6. The length of the upper arm is more than one foot, and that is how much height is being lost if players do not catch the ball with their arms fully extended.

JUMPING DRILLS

The same drill can be used to teach jumping for rebounds and extending the arms. Have players stand about three feet from the wall and throw the ball off the wall as though it were a shot. They then jump and catch the ball at the top of their jump. After they have mastered jumping, have them jump and catch the ball with their arms extended.

Here is a drill for teaching aggressiveness, moving to the ball, jumping, extending the arms, and protecting the ball (discussed below): Position two players about five feet from the backboard and to the left side of the rim. Throw the ball off the backboard without hitting the rim, so that it rebounds an equal distance from both players. They compete to get the ball. If you move the players farther from the basket, they will also be able to practice moving toward the basket to get the ball.

DEFENSIVE REBOUNDING

Protect the ball. Very often a player will bring down a defensive rebound and turn to

Figure 6.7. Protecting the ball after a rebound.

pass the ball to a teammate; the ball, held about waist high, will be promptly grabbed by an opposing player. To avoid this situation, the player must protect the ball.

To properly protect the ball, the rebounder, who is facing the basket, lands facing the basket and then pivots on her left foot within a range of about 90 degrees, keeping her back to the opposing players (Figure 6.7). She is bent at the knees and waist, crouched over the ball, and her elbows are out. She has a firm grasp on the ball with two hands. The ball is protected by her back on one side and her elbows on two sides; the narrow space between the player and the baseline helps protect her front side.

Finally, when the player pivots from side to side, contact is a threat to other players because her elbows are out.

Please note: it is within the rules to pivot with your elbows out as long as your arms are not swinging back and forth. If your arms are stationary and your body is moving, you are making space for yourself on the court and are within the rules. An opposing player who sees that he might catch an elbow in the chest or stomach probably won't have much interest in trying to strip the ball. This is not to say that you are intending to hurt another player but only to say that you are entitled to make space for yourself in this way, and if you do, other players will observe that and respect it.

Players who swing their arms, whether or not their bodies are moving, are committing a foul and, because of the speed that is generated, are likely to hurt an opponent. Players should be instructed not to swing their arms.

Block out. A player in a proper man-to-man defensive position will be between her man and the basket, with her back to the basket (Figure 6.8). Also, she will be shifted over to the ball side of the offensive player to have a chance to deflect any incoming pass. As soon as the shot goes up, instead of run-

Figure 6.8. The defender (in white) is shifted toward her left; she is about to pivot on her right foot.

Figure 6.9. As soon as another player shoots the ball, the defender pivots on her right foot to block out the offensive player.

ning toward the basket the player pivots 180 degrees on the foot closest to the opposing player (Figure 6.9). In doing so, the defensive player swings her body directly in front of the offensive player before the offensive player can move. Once this contact is made, the offensive player is unable to get around the defender and head for the basket. As soon as the contact is made, the defender can release that position and go for the rebound. If the defender is already in proper rebounding position, she simply holds the contact with the offensive player as long as possible while crouching to jump for the rebound.

OFFENSIVE REBOUNDING

Offensive rebounds offer excellent scoring opportunities. It is often difficult for a team

to work the ball inside offensively; grabbing offensive rebounds affords another way of getting the ball underneath for easy shots.

Offensive rebounding is drilled essentially the same way as defensive rebounding. When the shot is taken, the offensive rebounders go hard to the backboard and attempt to get the best rebounding position.

Against a zone defense, there are no specific defensive players assigned to block out offensive rebounders. One or more offensive players can be designated as an offensive rebounder; that is, they are not looking to score in the particular offense being used (such as the 1-2-2 closed offense discussed in Chapter 12). Instead, they move into the openings created as the defensive zone shifts from side to side. The weak side (the side of the court away from the ball) is often left

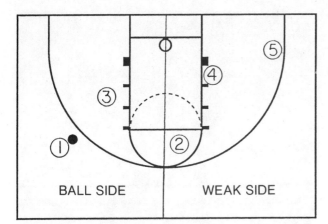

Figure 6.10. The weak side is the half of the court away from the ball.

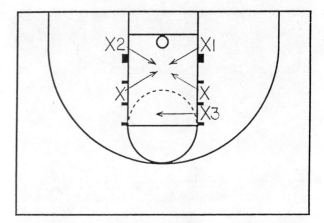

Figure 6.12. Positions of defensive players as foul shot is taken.

unguarded; a lot of rebounds come into that area as offensive shots bounce off the rim. The ball side and weak side are shown in Figure 6.10.

FOUL SHOTS

The players line up for a foul shot as shown in Figure 6.11. The defensive team is entitled to the closest position to the backboard on each side, and each team then alternates positions toward the foul line.

The defensive players attempt to block out the offensive players by quickly moving to the positions shown in Figure 6.12. Principally, the defensive players closest to the

basket (X1 and X2 in Figure 6.11) want to beat the offensive players O4 and O5 to the center of the area in front of the basket.

Offensive players should not always move toward the center when the ball is shot but should, at least a third of the time, move to the outside in an attempt to get the rebound. In Figure 6.13, O4 and O5 are making an outside move. When the offensive rebounders do this, the defenders have to hesitate and cannot move as quickly to block the middle area.

In order to move quickly into the lane after the ball has left the foul shooter's hands, the players drive off the outside foot toward the middle. For example, in Figure

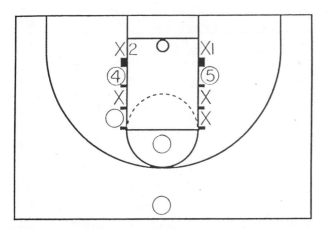

Figure 6.11. Position of the players before a foul shot.

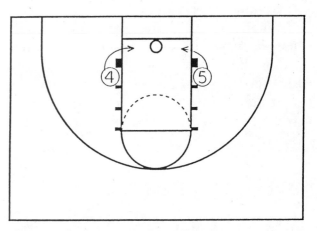

Figure 6.13. Rebounders O4 and O5 move to the outside to get rebound on a foul shot.

Figure 6.14. Both players push off the outside (right) foot, moving to get the inside position on a rebound of a foul shot.

Figure 6.15. The player in white pushes off his inside (left) foot, moving to get the outside position on a rebound of a foul shot.

6.14 each player drives to the middle by pushing off the ball of his right foot. When a player attempts to make an outside move from the right side of the basket, he pushes off his left foot to move down the line rather than toward the middle (Figure 6.15).

Finally, the defensive team should designate a player to step in front of the free-throw shooter. This prevents the free-throw shooter from getting the rebound of a shot that bounces off the front rim and back toward the foul line. The proper position is shown by X1 in Figure 6.12.

I don't spend a great deal of time drilling proper technique for rebounding after a foul shot because there isn't sufficient time. I do show the players the proper technique and drill it in one practice and then call fouls during scrimmages over the next few days so that the players get used to the proper movements. I then watch the players in scrimmages and in the games to be sure that they are blocking out. If not, I take additional time during practice to drill the proper technique.

7
PASSING AND SCREENING

CHEST PASS

The most frequently thrown pass is the chest pass. The body position for throwing the chest pass is shown in Figure 7.1: the passer's body is erect, the elbows are in at her sides, and the ball is held at chest height. The most common mistake passers make is starting with their elbows out (Figure 7.2). This takes the snap out of the pass, as the arms are not in the most efficient position to push the ball forward; it also decreases the accuracy of the pass.

The proper passing motion puts backspin on the ball to make it easy to catch and puts snap on the ball so that the pass is quick and harder to steal. It is important to stride forward toward the receiver as the pass is thrown. This puts the player's weight behind the ball.

Figure 7.1. The passer strides forward with her elbows in.

Figure 7.2. Incorrectly throwing a pass: the elbows are flying out.

Figure 7.3. The passer's hands grasp the ball symmetrically.

Figure 7.5. The hands start to rotate downward as they move forward, putting backspin on the ball.

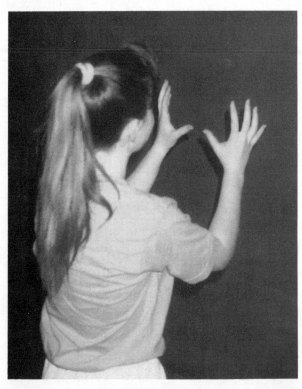

Figure 7.4. The correct hand action while throwing a pass: first, the hands point slightly upward as the pass starts.

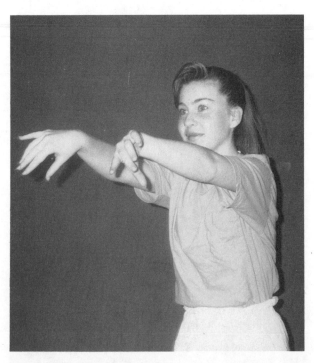

Figure 7.6. As the player follows through, the hands face downward and the wrists are limp.

The ball is grasped with both hands spread out and the thumbs in position as shown in Figure 7.3. Perhaps the best way to teach the proper motion is to emphasize the action of the thumbs. As the arms are moving forward just prior to releasing the ball, the thumbs hold their position on the basketball (Figure 7.4). As the basketball is released, each hand starts to rotate to the outside, which brings the thumbs forward and down (Figure 7.5). When the player follows through properly, the hands are fully bent at the wrists with the fingers pointing to the side (Figure 7.6).

DRILLS

Have the players line up in pairs facing each other. First, the players practice the proper passing motion without using the ball, focusing on the movement of their hands. Then they can add the proper position of the elbows to start the pass. Finally, they can add the forward stride. When the players can put the entire motion together without the ball, add the ball to the drill.

At this point, all of the drills on footwork described in Chapter 4 will also serve as good passing drills. The skills then can be worked into your scrimmages.

One of the most enjoyable drills for players is a little complicated to explain in writing, but it is easy to teach. Five players are positioned in a circle about the size of the circle around the foul line. (Figure 7.7) The position each player occupies has a number. Player 1 holds one ball to start the drill, and player 2 holds a second ball. All passes from players 2, 3, 4, and 5 are always thrown to player 1.

Player 1 starts the drill by passing to player 3. Player 2 then passes to player 1. This is the basis of the whole drill and it is simply repeated over and over with different players. Player 1 then passes to player 4 as player 3 passes back to player 1. Player 1

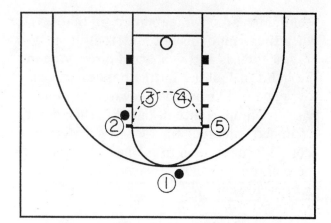

Figure 7.7. Positions for fast-passing drill.

passes to player 5, and player 4 passes to player 1.

The drill now reverses and changes slightly as the ball starts traveling back around the circle. When player 1 receives the pass from player 4, he returns it to player 4. Player 5 then passes to player 1, who in turn passes to player 3. Player 4 returns the ball to player 1, who passes to player 2. Player 3 returns the ball to player 1, and the first cycle has been completed.

The circle of players then rotates to the right, with player 2 becoming player 1, player 1 becoming player 5, player 5 becoming player 4, and so on. The drill is then repeated until each player has a chance to be player 1.

Start this drill very slowly, as with all drills, until the players get the hang of it. This drill requires concentration and proper passing skills.

Once the drill is learned, the two balls will really fly around the circle.

LOOK IN

An important component of most offenses is the pass from the perimeter (either by a guard or a forward) into the pivot area. When a player receives a pass in the triangle drill, as he squares to the triple-threat position he should look toward the basket as if looking for an open teammate. In that way, when the team drills add the frontline players, the guards and wings will already be in the habit of looking for the pass to a frontline player; that pass is known as the entry pass. The importance of this skill should not be underestimated: the key to successfully scoring from close in to the basket is getting the ball to the frontline players who are in a position to score.

BOUNCE PASS

The bounce pass is thrown with the same technique as the chest pass, except that the ball is bounced off the floor to the receiver (Figure 7.8). Proper technique is important

Figure 7.9. Throwing a bounce pass around the defender, using the left foot as the pivot foot.

Figure 7.8. The defender cannot bend to the side and downward quickly enough to deflect the bounce pass.

Figure 7.10. Throwing a bounce pass to the defender's left, again using the left foot as the pivot foot.

in the bounce pass for this reason: when the ball hits the floor, it picks up overspin, which makes it move faster, stay lower off the bounce, and become harder to grasp. With proper backspin, the ball comes up higher and softer; that results in fewer turnovers.

Another type of bounce pass is frequently used to pass the ball into the pivot, as shown in Figures 7.9 and 7.10. The idea is to step to the side to get a passing angle around the defender. The footwork is the same as the usual footwork for passing—that is, use the left foot as the pivot foot at all times. This skill will later be coupled with the frontline players' skills discussed in Chapter 9 as part of the team's offense.

The chest pass drill (Chapter 4) can be used to drill the bounce pass. Then have your passer work with a frontline player by passing the ball in as shown in Figure 7.11.

Figure 7.11. Throwing a bounce pass to a player in the post position.

BASEBALL PASS

The baseball pass is very useful for breaking a full-court press (see Chapter 14). I teach

this pass to only one or two of the players who have both strength and coordination. The ball is passed as a pitcher delivers a pitch, striding off the right foot onto the left foot. This is an exception to the footwork that the players have been taught, and for that reason it has to be carefully drilled.

The pass is thrown from out of bounds after a basket, a time-out, or a turnover; it can also be thrown from on court after the ball has been inbounded. In any case, the player is throwing the ball more than 10 or 15 yards and therefore needs additional power. The right foot is used as the pivot foot; the player then strides forward onto the left foot (Figure 7.12). She throws the overhand pass as shown in Figure 7.13, following through properly.

The baseball pass is frequently used against the full-court press by the offensive player who receives the inbounds pass, and proper footwork is essential. The player establishes the right foot as the pivot foot, pivots on that foot, and faces the length of the court. Now he is in position, without having walked, to throw the baseball pass. The technique is the same as when the pass is thrown from out of bounds.

Whether throwing the ball from out-of-bounds or inbounds, the passer should first practice throwing to a stationary teammate. When that skill has been learned, the passer should practice throwing the ball to a teammate who is cutting across the court. The players who are receiving the ball have to give the passer a proper angle. They will be trying to cut into the open court to catch the pass; in doing so, they must be careful not to run directly away or directly toward the passer. These are the most difficult passes to throw and catch: Running directly away from the passer, the receiver has difficulty in seeing the ball and judging its speed and distance. Running toward the passer makes the ball easier to see, but again it is difficult to judge speed and distance or make adjustments if the ball is thrown off line.

Figure 7.12. Throwing a baseball pass: the weight starts on the back foot and shifts forward as the player strides forward.

Figure 7.13. Releasing the baseball pass: the player throws the ball overhanded and follows through properly.

ONE PASS THAT SHOULD NEVER BE THROWN

A pass from one side of the court to the other is known as a crosscourt pass. In Figure 7.14, O5 is passing across the court to O3. If the pass is underthrown, it is easily stolen; if the pass is overthrown, it goes out of bounds. Even if the pass is completed, the offensive team is no better off having the ball on the other side of the court because the defense has time to shift back into position while the ball is in the air.

This pass is all risk and no gain, and for that reason it should never be thrown by a team playing at the elementary levels of the game. It is true that more advanced offensive

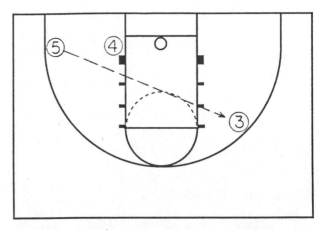

Figure 7.14. The crosscourt pass: a bad idea for beginners.

teams use this pass to move the ball quickly against an overshifted defense. These teams can shoot with accuracy from long distance and move the ball around the court with speed and precision. There is simply no reason to recommend this pass for teams without these advanced skills.

FAKES

When a pass is stolen, it is usually because the passer looks at the receiver before passing the ball. This gives the defender of the receiving player an opportunity to anticipate the pass and move into the passing lane. In order to avoid having passes stolen in this way, players must learn to disguise some of their passes by learning the ball fake, the eye fake, and the shot fake. The idea is to make defenders either freeze in their tracks or actually move in the wrong direction.

Ball fake. The player extends his arms as though he were going to pass the ball in one direction—to the right, for example—but does not stride or shift his weight in that direction. The player holds onto the ball, quickly draws the ball back in, strides, and passes left. In making the fake, the arms are mostly but not fully extended.

Figure 7.15. A head and eye fake to the right.

Eye fake, or head fake. Instead of striding to the left or to the right, the player strides straight forward toward the defender with his eyes in one direction while he passes the ball in the other direction (Figure 7.15).

Shot fake. The shot fake is similar to the ball fake, except that instead of faking a pass, the player fakes a one-handed shot. Again, the arms are not fully extended, but the ball is brought quickly upward as though the player were about to shoot. This skill enables the offensive player to freeze the defender and then start a drive to the basket. The player does not shift his weight but rather brings the ball down quickly after the fake and drives the ball to the basket. The shot fake is particularly effective after the offensive player has hit a shot from the outside. The defender is concerned that the player will again shoot the ball the next time down the court. Instruct your point guard to get the ball right back to that same player, who will then fake a shot and drive the ball to the hoop.

In the same manner, a player who has just driven to the basket successfully can fake a drive and be open for a jump shot. When your player has successfully completed one move, he has laid the foundation for the successful completion of a complementary move: shoot, then drive; or drive, then shoot.

Drills. All of the fakes can be drilled in the triangle drill discussed in Chapter 4.

SCREENS

Setting a screen allows a teammate to temporarily get free from his defender. A screener accomplishes this by placing his body in the way of his teammate's defender. The knees are somewhat flexed; the arms may be crossed against the player's chest. This position enables the player to absorb the impact of the expected collision with the defender.

Body position. The screener must be motionless when contact is made with the defensive player—the feet, arms, or body cannot be moving. The most frequent error is leaning into the defensive player as he is going by. Referees are quick to call screening fouls.

Where to set the screen. Coaches refer to screening as "head-hunting." This sounds more bloodthirsty than it is. The term is intended to emphasize the importance of looking for your teammate's defender and setting the screen right next to him. When a player looks to set a screen at a particular spot on the floor, anticipating that the defender will soon be arriving at that spot, the screen is usually not successful because the defender can go around the screener.

In Figure 7.16 player number 43 is in proper position to set a screen for the ball handler. As the ball handler passes her screening teammate, she brushes her shoulder; the defensive player must go around the

screener or trail behind the ball handler. In either case, the ball handler will have a one- or two-step advantage as she brushes by the screen.

Figure 7.17 shows an incorrect screen. The screener is too far from the defensive player whom she is attempting to screen. The player has room to squeeze between the ball handler and the screen.

The principles are the same whether you are screening for a teammate who has the ball or one who is cutting to get open for a pass. One caution: a screener may not position himself directly behind the offensive player whom he wishes to screen. The offensive player must allow the defender at least a one-step margin if the offensive player is directly behind the player he is seeking to screen.

Figure 7.16. The ball handler runs her defender into her teammate's screen.

Figure 7.17. The screener is too far from the defensive player, who fights through the screen.

ALL-PURPOSE DRILL

One drill that is useful for passing, cutting, screening, and breaking the press works this way: with four offensive players working against four defensive players, the offensive team passes the ball inbounds and must complete four passes without dribbling, committing a turnover, or having the ball stolen. This drill requires the players to work on the skills that are most essential to in-bounding the ball, breaking the press, moving to get open, protecting the ball, pivoting, and using the jump stop.

The offense is awarded one point if it completes four passes and a second point if it takes the ball the length of the court and scores a basket; the defense is awarded one point if it stops the offense from completing four passes, and a second point if it steals the ball.

8
DRIBBLING

All players need some dribbling skills. Each player should be able to take the ball to the basket from a standing position or after catching the ball on the run. Frontline players will also need some skill dribbling the ball to complete the drop-step and slide-down moves described in Chapter 9.

Most important, at least two guards must be able to dribble the ball up the court quickly with either hand without looking at the ball and be able to change directions quickly by shifting the ball to either hand.

Many opponents will use some form of a pressing defense, and, whether passing or dribbling the ball up the court, the guards will need to be able to take advantage of a one-on-one situation. If a guard cannot see a trap coming—that is, two defensive players moving toward him—because he is dribbling with his head down, chances are the ball will either be stolen outright or he will be trapped and forced into throwing a bad pass. When the ball is stolen either off the dribble or off a bad pass, the result is often an easy break-away lay-up. In games where the score only goes into the 20s or 30s or even the 40s, giving up two, three, or four baskets of this type can be devastating. A good deal of defensive effort is undermined by turning offensive possessions into baskets for the opposition.

During tryouts you'll note that most of your guards will have at least some ability to dribble the ball, but in almost all cases they will be watching the ball as they dribble. As with all skills, to teach dribbling properly you need to start at step 1 and not progress to the next step until players have mastered the preceding one. I explain to players that dribbling is a skill that can only be learned through repetition. If they dribble the ball a few hundred times per day in practice, or at home, in a month or two they can master the skill. Also, unless they put in the practice time, they won't significantly improve as a ball handler.

BODY POSITION

The higher the ball bounces, the greater the chance that it can be stolen. A player standing in place should be dribbling the ball no higher than halfway between the knee and the waist. In order to do that, the player must be in a crouched position (Figure 8.1): the knees are bent significantly, the back is almost straight, and the nondribbling hand is extended somewhat in front of the body to protect the ball. The ball is dribbled toward the back foot. This basic dribbling position serves to protect the ball from being stolen.

As the player goes into motion, the body

Figure 8.1. Head up, back straight, knees bent when dribbling the ball.

cannot be kept bent this low, and therefore the dribble will rise somewhat—but not above waist height. The ball moves farther forward until it is just ahead of the body and toward the side of the dribbling hand when the player is in full stride.

HAND POSITION

The hand should be spread out on the ball; the ball is controlled with the fingertips and should not hit the palm. For best control, the dribbler actually touches the ball while it is still rising: the fingers are on the ball, gaining control, in the last few inches of the ball's rise off the floor. Touching the ball late in the dribble, when it is on the way down, is more like slapping it than dribbling it, and

results in the loss of a good deal of control of the dribble.

THE CROSSOVER DRIBBLE

Imagine a player dribbling a zigzag pattern up the court. As she starts to her left, she dribbles with her left hand, her body between the ball and the defender (Figure 8.2). To switch directions, she must bring the ball back very close to her body and transfer the ball to her right hand with a low quick bounce called the crossover dribble: the left hand catches the ball on the way up, before it reaches its full height, and dribbles it over to the right hand. As the player moves to her right, she again positions her body between the ball and the defender so the defender cannot reach out and steal the ball or flick it away.

Figure 8.2. The dribbler protects the ball by keeping her body between the ball and the defender.

Two natural tendencies should be avoided when making the crossover dribble:

▶ Because many players don't feel comfortable maneuvering the ball with their nondominant hand, they will reach across with their dominant hand to bring the ball over (Figure 8.3) instead of bouncing the ball from hand to hand. Reaching over puts them in danger of losing the ball by dribbling it off their foot or by being out of balance. It also takes longer and has less control.

▶ When a ball is bounced sideways from one hand to the other, it will tend to acquire sidespin. This makes the ball bounce off the floor low and away from the receiving hand. To avoid this tendency, players should put backspin on the ball on the crossover dribble so it comes up at a less severe angle and is not spinning away from them.

DRILLS

While you are illustrating the basic dribbling technique, you should be the only one holding the basketball. If your players are holding basketballs at this point, your voice will quickly be drowned out by the sound of bouncing basketballs. After you have finished your illustration, give each of the players a ball and then have them line up in a straight line a few feet apart.

The players simply dribble the ball in place while you walk up and down the line getting them into the proper position. This is the time to break players of their habit of looking at the ball while dribbling. If they can't control the dribble without looking at the ball at this point, they certainly won't be able to do so once they start moving.

Players start this drill with the nondominant hand, usually the left hand. After about a hundred dribbles, let them rest for a moment and then do the same with the dominant hand. The drill should be repeated with the left hand, the right hand, and then the left hand again, so that the players dribble the ball three hundred times with their nondominant hand and two hundred times with their dominant hand during each practice. After a few practice sessions, they are ready to start walking the ball up the court. Have them go up and back three times with the left hand and then switch to the right hand, repeating the process two or three times.

Next, have the players jog slowly up the court. Tell them that as soon as they can dribble the length of the court and back twice without losing control of the dribble, they can move up to the next level until they eventually achieve full running speed.

If you are fortunate enough to have one or

Figure 8.3. The crossover dribble: incorrectly reaching for the ball.

more players who have already mastered these initial skills, they can separately do the more advanced drills that follow. After you have made sure that each player is dribbling properly, the captains can run the rest of the team through more of the basic drills while you take time with each of your advanced players to determine what level of drills will advance their skills. Just don't miss any of the steps along the way.

There are several ways to make these dribbling drills more interesting. Once the players are jogging, they can shoot lay-ups at the far end of the court. Make sure that they approach the basket at a 45-degree angle. This is a good time for them to learn to slow up during the last two or three steps so that they are under control taking the lay-up.

Players enjoy relay races, but they often lose control of the dribble by going too fast. That can be corrected somewhat by requiring them to go back to the point where they lost control and start again before finishing their leg of the relay.

I use two games to help break up the monotony. "Dribble War" starts out with each player dribbling a ball inside specified boundaries—initially, the entire area that is inbounds and inside the three-point line. Players are eliminated when they lose their dribble or step out of the specified area of the court. They simultaneously try to keep their dribble going and knock away the opponent's ball. The point of the game is to encourage players to look up while they dribble.

As the number of players grows smaller, so do the boundaries of the drill. After four or five players are knocked out, the area is cut in half. When only two or three players are left, the paint area can also be eliminated. The last remaining dribbler wins.

"Possessed" starts out with each player holding a ball, standing on the baseline, and facing the far end of the court. One player, who is "Possessed," initially faces all of the other players. The players begin dribbling the length of the court. If any player has his dribble knocked away by the player who is "Possessed" or loses his dribble, that player also becomes "possessed" and joins the defender. Again, the last remaining dribbler is the winner.

As a practical matter, I don't have my front line spend much time practicing these skills, because I would rather have them spend the vast majority of their practice time on the skills they will need to use most in game situations. So I divide the squad between guards and forwards, giving the forwards only abbreviated versions of all the dribbling skills.

When the players can dribble up and down the court at least at a jogging pace, I introduce the concept of changing hands while dribbling. I start them dribbling hand to hand in place and then while jogging. Once they have the idea of changing hands, place some cones (or boxes or chairs) out on the court at regular intervals of about 15 feet. The players are in a line, each holding a ball. Players dribble to the right of the first cone using the right hand and then switch hands, dribbling to the left of the second cone using the left hand, and so on (Figure 8.4).

Players running this drill usually want to go too fast too soon; be sure that they are under control. Also, they tend to change hands too late in the crossover process; if the cones were defenders they could reach out and steal the ball or flick it away during the switch of hands. To avoid this the crossover should occur as soon as dribblers pass one cone and before they are in range of the next cone (Figure 8.5). Later on, use live defenders who can use their arms but not move their feet; then allow them to defend by maintaining one pivot foot. Next, have the line of defenders hold their spacing but advance as players try to dribble through them. This last drill is excellent practice but is usually difficult to organize and maintain.

Figure 8.4. The cone drill.

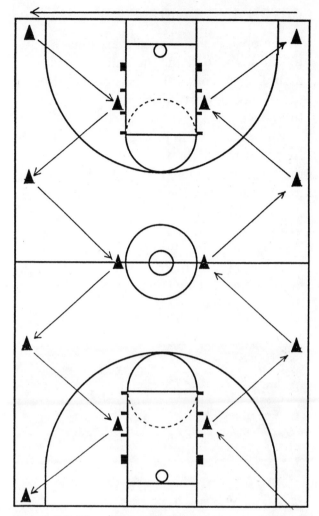

Figure 8.6. The zigzag dribbling drill.

As time allows, place defenders in broken, irregular formations and have them come at the dribbler who is attempting to move the ball up the court. This is good practice for avoiding traps and breaking the full-court press.

Another variation is to place cones as shown in Figure 8.6. The players line up in one corner of the court and follow a pattern shown by the arrows. Dribblers go to the first cone using the left hand, change hands as in the first cone drill, and dribble to the second cone using the right hand. This is repeated around the court. Dribblers use the same hand as the direction in which they are moving.

Figure 8.5. The dribbler switches hands before reaching the "defender."

CATCH AND DRIBBLE

In the open court, your players must be able to catch the ball on the run and continue dribbling upcourt. This situation arises on fast-break opportunities and also against a full-court press.

When players catch the ball on the run, the first foot to hit the floor becomes the pivot foot; the ball must be dribbled before the pivot foot leaves the ground. Inexperienced players will often take too many steps before dribbling the ball, resulting in a turnover. The skill is drilled by having players catch a baseball pass on the run, get the ball on the ground quickly to start their dribble, and drive to the basket for a lay-up.

Figure 8.8. The dribbler spins away from the defender by pivoting on her right foot and continues upcourt, dribbling with her left hand.

THE SPIN MOVE

Dribblers use the spin move to avoid being forced in one direction until they run out of court and then picking up their dribble in the worst possible position. The spin move allows dribblers to change directions without switching hands in front of their bodies. It is also useful for driving in the open court or driving the ball to the basket, especially along the baseline.

The spin move is illustrated by dribbling the ball at an angle toward the right sideline, as shown in Figure 8.7. Just before reaching

Figure 8.7. The dribbler, stopped at the sideline by her defender, protects the ball near her back foot.

the sideline, the dribbler plants her left foot while continuing the dribble with the ball back toward the right foot. This serves to protect the ball from the defender's reach. The player then pivots to the right (clockwise) on her right foot and, on the return bounce, continues the dribble with her left hand. She is now facing the left sideline at an angle so that she can continue to move the ball upcourt (Figure 8.8).

From the left side, the dribbler plants the right foot, pivots to the left (counterclockwise), and continues the dribble with the right hand. In other words, if you're dribbling with the right hand, you plant your left foot; if you're dribbling with the left hand, you plant your right foot.

First, walk the players through this drill and have them repeat it until you're certain they can do it. The players can then run the cone drill illustrated in Figure 8.6 and, when they approach each cone, switch hands by using the spin move rather than the crossover dribble.

The spin move should also be practiced in the open court where the players continue in essentially a straight line. In effect, dribblers offer the ball with the right hand and then switch with a spin at the last moment as they go by the defender.

9
ATTACKING THE BASKET

DRIVING

The first step in driving to the basket is to be set in the triple-threat position. The footwork for receiving a pass and squaring to the basket in the triple-threat position is discussed in Chapter 4.

The player starts the drive to the right by executing either a pass fake to the left (Figure 9.1) or a shot fake as she pushes to the right off the ball of her left foot. She protects the ball by bringing it close to and across her body (Figure 9.2) and dribbles with her right hand before her pivot foot leaves the ground (Figure 9.3). The offensive player cuts past the defender with only a few inches separating them, continues to the basket, and shoots the lay-up off the backboard.

By the time you are teaching players to drive, they should have no trouble getting the ball into the triple-threat position. The first drill therefore involves isolating the long first step with the right leg, as that is the most important part of the drive.

Players set up in the correct position at approximately a 45-degree angle to the basket, even with the top of the key. Place three pieces of tape on the floor—the first two to show the starting position of the left and right foot, the third to show where the first step of the right foot should land. Stand in front of the players so they get the feel of

taking the first step past a defender. They need not fake, protect the ball, dribble, or continue to the basket at this stage. The most frequent error is to take the first step well to the side of the defender; that cuts down the effectiveness of the drive, as the defender has more time to recover, and it takes the driver longer to go around the defender.

After players are able to take that first step, add dribbling to the drill. Be sure the dribble starts before the pivot foot moves. The players can then continue to the basket and take a lay-up before getting back in line. The team can then be divided into two or three groups who can practice this part of the drill at different baskets.

The next component to add is the pass fake or the shot fake, described in Chapter 7. Players should protect the ball after a ball fake by bringing it in close to the body and low to the ground while moving it from the left side to the right; on a shot fake, they should bring the ball down quickly and again close to the body.

Another frequent error is to try to shoot the ball off the backboard from an angle that is either greater or less than 45 degrees. Make them work on getting the 45-degree angle right. It helps at first to put some tape on the court to show them the way to the basket.

Figure 9.1. The player fakes to the left while pushing off her left foot to start driving right.

Figure 9.2. She protects the ball by keeping it close to her body when bringing it from left to right as she starts driving to the basket.

Once the players can drive the ball correctly from a 45-degree angle, have them practice the same drill driving the baseline and then driving straight down the middle of the court. An easy, consistent rule to follow is this: players should shoot the ball straight into the basket without using the backboard except when at a 45-degree angle to the basket—from that angle, they should always use the backboard.

Driving the ball to the left starts from the same triple-threat position, but there are two differences: first, the long first step with the right foot is in front of the pivot foot as the right foot crosses in front of the body (Figure 9.4); second, the dribble begins and continues with the left hand all the way to the basket.

I allow players who have not mastered the lay-up with the left hand to continue to use the right hand even from the left side. Once the players are proficient in making the lay-up with the right hand, I have them start practicing left-handed lay-ups. Otherwise, the drills are the same for the drive to the left.

POWER MOVES

Beginning basketball players hit very few shots from the outside. A few times each season, I have a volunteer keep a chart using a diagram of the basketball court. The volunteer marks a circle on the chart at the point where each shot was taken and puts an X through the circle for each basket. Each

Figure 9.3. She starts the dribble before her pivot foot leaves the ground.

Figure 9.4. Driving to the basket: the first step to the left.

year the charts show the same story: most of the baskets are made inside. In fact, outside shooting (from at least as far as the foul line) results in baskets only about 15 percent to 20 percent of the time. Most of the scoring comes from successfully working the ball inside or from offensive rebounds. So the basic idea is to teach your team how to move the ball inside and how to score from there.

Players often become confused when they have too many moves to learn. It is therefore best to teach one basic power move to the basket. Players should learn the same move from the opposite side of the basket for this reason: most players prefer to use their right hand, and there is a danger that the offense will be restricted to the right side of the court. The defense can adjust by packing

that side with defenders; when the offense moves in the same direction each time, it becomes easier for the defense to steal the ball. When players learn to make a move from the left side, even if they shoot with the wrong hand, the offense can operate from both sides of the court.

POSITION

Where. The most common position to receive a pass is just outside the paint about six to eight feet from the basket. The player is close enough to attack the basket but is outside of the three-second area. If a player receives the pass inside the paint, it will usually take one or two seconds for the ball to reach the player and another second or two before he can shoot it. The risk of a three-second violation is high.

How. The offensive player wants to arrive at the designated spot ahead of the defender. In order to do so, he can start from any position in the area and execute an appropriate fake and cut. For example, he can start even with the basket on the same side as the spot he wishes to receive the ball and cut across the paint and back to the spot (Figure 9.5). A good fake and cut leaves the offensive player a step ahead of the defender. The defender is then moving toward the offensive player as he catches the ball. That makes it harder to protect against a move to the hoop.

Figure 9.6. The offensive player, in black, is in the post position and ready to receive the ball. His base is wide and his knees are bent as he signals for the ball to be thrown on the side away from the defender.

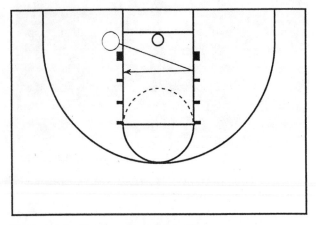

Figure 9.5. Cutting to get position.

Drill your team in simply cutting to the right spot. Have your players execute a variety of good fakes and sharp cuts to get to the proper position. At first this drill should be done without a defender, and then with light defense, and finally with full defense.

The offensive player has a wide stance with arms partially extended (Figure 9.6) in order to take up as much space as possible on the court; this prevents the defender from reaching around and batting the pass away. His knees are bent to provide stability so he can't be pushed out of the way. He signals for the pass with the hand farthest away from the defender.

Have players get into proper position and signal for the ball. At first run this drill without a defender and then with light defense, with the defensive players at times being on the left side of players and at times on the right side; finally, drill the technique against a full defense.

When. Good timing by the post player is essential; it doesn't accomplish anything for the post player to arrive at the proper location when the ball is on the other side of the court. The post player has to time his move to start as the ball is being passed to the guard or forward who will be in position to pass it to him. While the post player is making his cut and getting into position, the perimeter player is receiving the ball, setting to the triple-threat position, and looking to pass the ball inside.

This technique can be drilled first with three offensive players in the positions shown in Figure 9.7. The ball can be passed to the frontline player by either O2 or O5. Then repeat the drill with light defensive pressure and finally with full defensive pressure. Be sure that the defenders of O2 and O5 do not anticipate the pass by immediately collapsing toward O4 to prevent the pass.

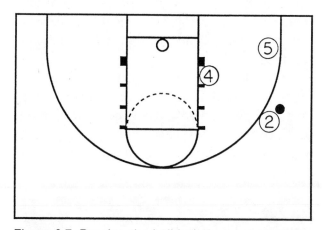

Figure 9.7. Passing the ball into the post position.

Footwork. Once offensive players have mastered the left-foot pivot, they can learn to catch the ball with both feet on the ground or in the air and land in the jump-stop position. That way, they are free to use either foot for a pivot foot.

Now your frontline player has received the ball; his back is to the basket and there is probably a defender either in a good defensive position or just a step away. The following sections consist of specific moves for the frontline player to get open for a good shot.

SPIN

A player who has received the ball in the pivot area with his back to the basket can make a spin move. Right-handers spin 180 degrees on their left foot. The player already has a wide base to receive the ball and keeps

the wide base in executing the move. This enables him to move the ball to the side of his defensive player. The player then takes a jump shot.

Figure 9.8 shows a player who has just received the ball; in Figure 9.9 she is in the process of executing the spin move; and in Figure 9.10 she completes the spin move and is ready to take a jump shot.

Note that by spinning on her left foot, the player keeps her body between the defender and the ball. In order to block the shot, the defender must move quickly to the side, get set, and jump. If the offensive player were to spin on her right foot, the ball would be within reaching distance of the defender, who would not need to move her feet to block the shot.

The spin move can be used on either side of the basket. The right-hander spins toward the basket from the right side of the court and away from the basket from the left side.

Figure 9.8. The spin move: the player has just received the ball.

Figure 9.9. She pivots on her left foot onto a wide base to get away from the defender.

Figure 9.10. The player completes the move by preparing to take a jump shot.

DROP STEP

One way of teaching someone to dance is to put actual footprints on the floor to illustrate the proper steps. This is a good way to teach the drop step, a relatively uncomplicated but very effective move.

The player starts on the right side of the basket in the position shown in Figure 9.11. The right foot is used as the pivot foot. The first step is with the left foot toward the basket: she steps into the paint, her left foot turning 90 degrees as she steps, and starts turning to the hoop (Figure 9.12). As she does so, she dribbles the ball once with her right hand.

As her left foot hits the ground, the player picks up the dribble and executes a jump shot, jumping off of the left foot and landing on both feet. That leaves her at a 45-degree angle, in lay-up position, and in proper bal-

Figure 9.11. The drop step: the player receives the ball just outside of the key.

Figure 9.12. Her first step is toward the hoop as she dribbles the ball once; her left foot and shoulders have turned 90 degrees.

Figure 9.13. She picks up the dribble and turns 45 degrees more into a jump stop.

ance (Figure 9.13). She then jumps straight up and shoots the ball off the backboard into the basket.

Note that the first step serves to seal off the defender: the offensive player has now positioned herself so that her body is mostly between the defender and the basket, giving her an undefended path to the hoop.

The drop-step move from the left side is the same, except that the player is using the left foot as the pivot foot. She steps toward the basket with her right foot and dribbles the ball once with her left hand. This is followed again by the jump stop and the close-in jump shot, preferably with the left hand.

Once a player can shoot the ball at least somewhat with her left hand, a good drill for making the shot a natural one works this

way: the player first takes a point-blank jump shot off the backboard from the right side; she moves under the basket to catch her own rebound and then moves to point-blank range on the left side. She then takes the same shot from the left side with the left hand, catches her rebound, and moves to the right side to shoot again with her right hand. A player should be able to do this drill in sequences of 10.

The drop-step move can also be made in the opposite direction from either side of the basket. From the left side, the right foot is the pivot foot; the player makes the first step into the paint to his left with his left foot (Figure 9.14), dribbles the ball once with his right hand, picks the ball up as his left foot hits the ground, and moves toward a jump

Figure 9.14. The drop step also can be used to move sideways into the lane.

Figure 9.15. The jump stop leaves the player directly in front of the basket.

stop. This puts him directly in front of the basket, about eight feet away (Figure 9.15). This move is used when the defensive player has overshifted to the offensive player's right. The move is more difficult to execute against a zone because there will often be another defensive player blocking the middle of the court.

The drop-step move in the opposite direction should not be taught until players have mastered going to the basket from the right side and the left side. Otherwise, it is apt to confuse them. Ideally, this move should be taught to players who have already learned the drop-step move from both sides the previous year.

SLIDE DOWN

The slide-down move is essentially the same as the drop-step move except that the player does not come into the paint. From the same starting position (Figure 9.11), the first step is down the line (Figure 9.16), with one dribble; the jump-stop technique is the same. However, at the conclusion of the jump stop, the player ends up directly facing the basket (Figure 9.17) at the foul lane at 0 degrees.

In order to accomplish this move, the player must twist about 90 degrees in the air during the jump stop. The most frequent error is to not bring the body around so that it is square to the basket at the end of the

Figure 9.16. Slide down: the first step and dribble down the line.

Figure 9.17. During the jump stop, the player turns another 90 degrees and lands facing the basket ready to shoot.

jump stop; the player then compensates by twisting in the air during the jump shot to complete. This makes the shot a lot harder to hit.

When drilling this move, don't let the players shoot the ball at first; drill the steps so that the player is in the proper triple-threat position at the conclusion of the jump stop. Then add the shot to the drill. This drill is best run straight down the lane from either the left or right side.

POWERING THE BALL TO THE HOOP

Two or three times each game your frontline players should either catch a pass or grab an offensive rebound and find themselves with an open lane four to six feet from the basket. The natural inclination is to shoot the ball where it is caught. Because players are going

to shoot a much higher percentage of lay-ups than short jump shots, they need to learn to power the ball to the basket.

Players should take one step with the left foot and shoot the lay-up with the right hand if they are going down the center or the right side; from the left side, they should take the step with the right foot and shoot the lay-up with the left hand.

Drill this skill first by having players catch the ball and make the same move 10 times each from the right and left sides and center of the court. This is a basic drill for any player learning a lay-up; no dribbling is necessary, as the player is allowed one step as long as the shot is taken before the pivot foot

Figure 9.18. The extra step: the player has picked up his dribble or received a pass.

Figure 9.19. He steps to the basket with his left foot and pivots on the left foot without dribbling.

hits the ground again. The players then can practice this skill by throwing the ball off the backboard without hitting the rim and catching the ball in a jump-stop position. Again, the drill is repeated 10 times from each of the three positions.

THE EXTRA STEP

Often a frontline player will get the ball somewhere near the basket but will be well guarded by one or two defenders. I expect my players to look at that situation as a scoring opportunity. The team works very hard to get the ball into an offensive player's hands near the basket; and when they do so, they want that player to shoot the ball almost every time.

The offensive player is not in a position to bring the ball up into shooting position due to the defensive coverage; he can, however, take advantage of the extra step that is allowed when you are shooting the ball. Assume that the offensive player has not yet established a pivot foot. The right-handed player takes a long step, moving closer to the basket with his left foot, and shoots the ball underhanded with his right hand (Figures 9.18–9.20).

It's hard to explain this concept to players, but it's very easy to illustrate. With a long first step and an underhand shot, they can easily cover seven or eight feet so that the shot is essentially a lay-up. It's true that they may be somewhat off balance or approaching the basket at an odd angle, but they will

Figure 9.20. The player completes his turn and shoots an underhand lay-up.

usually be able to get the shot off with a soft touch (because it will be underhand) and will very often be fouled while doing so. The foul will occur because the defensive players are off balance and are more likely to reach in to block the shot.

This can get the other team's taller players in foul trouble and can put your players on the foul line. When the shot is taken underhand, the defensive player rarely reaches the ball but instead hacks the offensive player on the arm. Since the arm is moving upward anyway, the elbow bends and the shot gets off in many instances, so there is a real chance for a three-point play with a foul on the opposing team's center to boot.

This skill can best be drilled by having players stand alone near the basket at various locations; they pivot once or twice and then take a long step toward the basket and shoot the ball underhanded. The drill can then be repeated adding light defensive pressure and then heavy defensive pressure. This move can be made more effective if players add a head fake or ball fake as well.

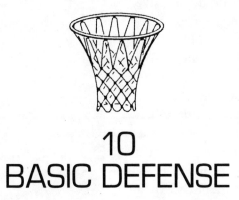

10
BASIC DEFENSE

Defense wins games; but at the start of the season your players won't care much about defense. They would rather just shoot the ball at both ends of the court if that were possible.

You have to sell them on the importance of defense. There are several ways to do that. I start out by having one of the best defensive players from the varsity team guard my incoming freshmen, one at a time, for a few plays in a scrimmage. After the scrimmage is over, I ask each of the players in turn to tell the team how it felt to be guarded by an excellent defender.

The players usually agree that they felt as if they had no chance to score.

At this point, I tell the team that each player has the opportunity to become a dominating defensive player, that they can make an offensive player feel that she has no chance to score. I emphasize that nothing they can do is more important to the success of the team than for them to play solid defense.

I then tell them that being able to play good defense is a prerequisite to getting playing time: the better defense they are playing, the more playing time they will get. I try to disabuse them of the notion that they can race around on offense and use defense as a time to rest.

Before teaching specific defensive skills, I set up a shooting contest between player 1, who is 5 feet from the basket, and player 2, who is 20 feet from the basket. I tell the players that we are going to give each player 10 shots and see who is the better shooter.

Somebody usually points out that the contest isn't fair because one player is much closer to the basket. I ask, "Why is it unfair?" to elicit the response that the closer you are to the basket, the easier it is to score.

This brings me to the principal object of defense: do not allow the other team to shoot from close to the basket. It doesn't make any difference whether you are playing a zone defense, a man-to-man defense, or any other kind of defense. If your team is consistently shooting from close to the basket and the other team is consistently shooting from the perimeter, your team will win most of its games.

I start the season by emphasizing the obligation of each player to protect the basket, and I keep emphasizing that as the season progresses. For example, if the offensive point guard is driving to the basket for a layup, it doesn't do your team any good at all for your center to keep his proper position on the offensive team's center. Protecting the basket must be every player's primary objective.

THE MAN-TO-MAN DEFENSE

Players cannot master the more complicated defenses until they've learned basic defensive skills. It is always best with beginning players to keep it simple and use one of the two basic defenses: zone or man-to-man (also called player-to-player).

The advantages of the zone defense are that you can put it in place without much practice time and that the area close to the basket is well protected. However, it is not a good choice for players who do not already have sound defensive fundamentals. In a zone defense, how is the defensive player to guard an opponent who comes into his zone? The answer is that he must employ basic man-to-man skills. These skills include proper body posture and a knowledge of where to play the opponent relative to the location of the ball and the basket. To play a good zone, a player must be competent in man-to-man defense.

That being the case, man-to-man defense is the place to start. Otherwise, the basic man-to-man defensive skills can be overlooked, and without these fundamental building blocks, defensive breakdowns are sure to occur. Also, because a man-to-man defense emphasizes the most basic aspects of the game, it provides your players with the best foundation for future improvement.

It is easier to sell players on a man-to-man defense once they see the personal challenge in guarding one particular person on the court and trying to stop that person from scoring. The man-to-man defense also provides greater opportunities for a team to steal the ball from the opposing guards and take it the length of the court for an uncontested basket.

The man-to-man defense is also a good first step toward more sophisticated defenses, such as a ball-pressure defense or a pressing defense. A simplified ball-pressure defense is a very effective, more complex version of a man-to-man defense and is a natural second

Figure 10.1. The proper defensive stance: knees bent, weight forward, and palms up.

step after the fundamentals have been properly learned. In my opinion, it is the most effective defense for any team below the varsity level. The ball-pressure defense is discussed in Chapter 11.

Proper body position. The proper defensive body position is up on the balls of the feet, knees bent, legs apart approximately shoulder width, and arms partially raised (Figure 10.1).

Defensive footwork. In moving from side to side, the feet do not meet, nor do they cross. Instead, the player takes a series of short, low, choppy steps. This style of defending allows the defensive player to react quickly to a change in direction by the offensive player.

In turning to the side, the player pivots on the opposite foot. For example, in turning to the right, he pivots on the ball of the left foot

Figure 10.2. The defender pivots on his left foot to turn to the right.

and resumes sliding to the right (Figure 10.2).

DRILL

To drill the basic defensive posture, have players stand in the proper position in three or four rows facing you. By signaling directions with your hand, have them slide to the left, for example, and then to the right, and so on. Run the drill first from side to side only. When the players have done that for two minutes, give them a short rest. Start side to side again and then incorporate 45-degree turns, again by hand signal, for another two minutes.

Distance from the offensive player. When the offensive player does not have the ball, a comfortable distance for the defender is approximately two to three feet. This allows the

defensive player sufficient time to react to movement by the offensive player.

The defender is shifted about one foot toward the ball side of the player he is guarding. This positions the defender to move quickly into the passing lane to steal or deflect a poor pass.

When the offensive player has the ball, the distance really depends upon the defender's skill and the location of the ball on the court. For example, if an offensive player has the ball underneath the basket, the defender should be just a few inches away. If the offensive player has the ball on the outside and you want to encourage the player to shoot, the defender should remain four or five feet away. If you want to be sure that the offensive player doesn't drive, the defender should remain three or four feet away or more. When you want to try to stop the outside shot, the defender should be about a foot from the offensive player.

Stay between your man and the basket. The defender should position himself with his back to the basket and stay between the man he is guarding and the basket. This sounds easy, but it is the one aspect that seems to give inexperienced defenders the most trouble. Players tend to watch the ball and lose track of their opponents. A useful drill is to have an offensive player move all around the court without the ball, staying within 20 feet of the basket; the defensive player must maintain proper position between the opponent and the basket.

Don't go too far from the basket. The next principle, not straying too far from the basket, can be best illustrated by drawing a semicircular chalk line that indicates the effective shooting range of the opposing team. The players should be advised, assuming a basic man-to-man defense is being used, not to go outside of that area. That encourages the other team to shoot from the outside. When the offensive player starts into the shooting position, the defender should put up his hand and move toward the offensive player. The idea is not to block the shot but rather to serve as a distraction; players shoot a lower percentage against defenders who have their hands up.

Again, the object is for your team to be shooting from close to the basket and the other team to be shooting from farther away. Many offenses are designed to lure the defensive players out past the three-point line; the offense is then in a position to drive the ball to the basket or pass it in to its frontline players. When the defense is overstretched, it is difficult to fulfill the basic function of protecting the basket.

Keep track of your man and the ball. Defenders must keep track of both the players they are guarding and the ball. They do this by frequently looking back and forth between the two. When they only watch the players they are guarding, they cannot help out teammates when another opponent breaks free. On the other hand, when they focus only on the ball, their offensive player is then free to cut toward the basket without a defender and receive a pass for a lay-up.

The most difficult pass to defend is the pass over the defender's head. The defender tends to turn around and look at the ball, losing track of the offensive player. The offensive player who has passed the ball then can cut toward the basket for a give-and-go lay-up. As part of the shell drill, which is described below, pay particular attention to having the offensive players throw passes over the heads of their defenders and cut toward the basket.

DRILLS

One-on-one drill. One defensive player starts at the top of the foul circle guarded by one defensive player. The offensive player tries to dribble the ball toward the basket; the defender is required to keep the offensive player out of the paint by using proper footwork. To insure that the defensive players do not reach in with their hands (as most defensive players will do instead of moving their feet to obtain correct body position), they must keep their hands behind their backs. Allow each offensive player about ten or fifteen seconds to get the ball into the paint.

While it is efficient to pair the players into six groups of two, for example, so that all can be practicing the skill at once, the drill loses its effectiveness when that is done. You should only use players who are at least adequate dribblers on offense. But, most likely, you will have only one, two, or, at most, three players who can dribble the ball well enough to require defenders to exercise good footwork. As they will tire quickly, it is hard to run too many repetitions of this drill. However, this drill is your best insurance against driving lay-ups by your opponents; for that reason, run it frequently but for short periods of time.

Zigzag drill. The players are confined to an area one-half the width of the court. The offensive player starts off dribbling to the left with the left hand; when he reaches the imaginary boundary at center court, he switches the ball to his right hand and continues on a diagonal to the right sideline. The defender stays in the basic defensive position with proper footwork, maintaining the proper distance and proper posture.

The players form a zigzag pattern in traveling the length of the court. They then change positions and come back on the other half of the court, again forming a zigzag pattern (Figure 10.3). This drill is good for practicing offensive as well as defensive skills.

Shell drill. The basic shell drill is the best drill I have seen for illustrating how a defense should work. The offense sets up in a 1-2-2 position on the court. The defenders then take their proper positions. The ball is simply passed around the perimeter, but not across the court, and the defensive players maintain the proper posture and position.

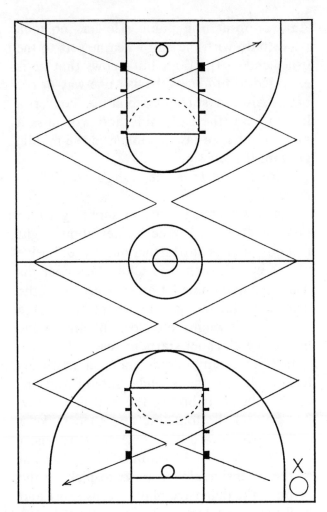

Figure 10.3. One-on-one zigzag drill.

During this drill, you can illustrate how the players should collapse on the center if the ball is passed into the middle.

Run this drill very slowly at first until everyone is clear what their defensive positions should be. After each pass, stop the movement of the players and check to see that each is in the correct defensive position. If anyone is out of position, ask the team who is out of position and what the proper position should be.

You can add motion to the drill by having the offensive player with the ball pass over the head of the defender and cut to the basket.

The offense can then go into a 2-1-2 alignment and follow the same routine.

COMMUNICATION

For the defense to be effective, the players should talk to each other. Each trip down the court, one defender should call out, "I've got the ball." If no one does that, another defender should ask, "Who's got the ball?" If there is no immediate answer, the defender closest to the ball should switch to defend against the dribbler.

Many times, a defender will not be able to see that he is about to be screened from the side or rear. A teammate must call out these screens: "Fred! Screen left!"

There are many other situations where communication is essential. On a fast break with two or more defenders back, for example, someone must take charge and organize the defense: "I've got the ball—you get the first pass," or "Open man on the right" when an offensive player breaks free.

Your players may be reluctant to talk out loud on defense; insist that they do.

DEFENSE AGAINST THE FAST BREAK

Assume that one of your guards (X) is passing to the other guard, and the ball is stolen at the point shown in Figure 10.4. Your team is now on defense, and the three players who

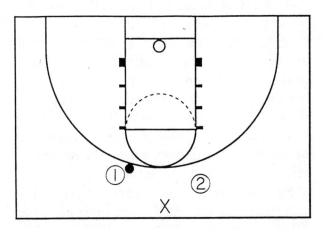

Figure 10.4. The last defender must retreat quickly to defend against a fast break.

are closest to your basket are two members of the opposing team (O1 has the ball) and only one defender (your guard who threw the pass that was stolen). If your guard rushes toward the player who has the ball, he will simply throw it over your guard's head to O2 for a breakaway lay-up. Likewise, if your guard holds his ground, both offensive players will sweep right by him.

When the guard tries to defend in the open court, there is far too much space to cover. It's no mystery where the ball is going—it's headed for your basket. Obviously, your guard has to retreat. When he gets into position near the basket, the situation has changed: now the offensive players must come to the defender in a much narrower space if they wish to get off a shot from close to your basket.

Although in this type of situation you will be outnumbered—by two to one, three to one, three to two, four to one, four to two, or four to three—the basic principle remains the same: forget about the ball, turn, run back to your basket as quickly as possible, and get into proper defensive position. It makes no difference how many offensive players there are or how many defensive players there are. As soon as the ball changes hands and the other team is pushing the ball up the court quickly, the defenders must fall back quickly and reorganize.

This lesson must be impressed especially upon your point guard. At times the other team will release a player on defense as soon as your team takes a shot; your point guard must be able to cover that player. Your number two guard must get back as quickly as possible for the same reason. This is particularly true if your point guard is penetrating or shooting, as it places primary defensive responsibility on your second guard.

Surprisingly, fast breaks are not very difficult to defend against. For the most part, the offensive player who is coming down the court is often, at this level of basketball, in a

state approaching panic. He has no idea what to do with the ball when he gets to the other end of the floor but knows that he is expected to produce a basket one way or the other. Also, most teams can at best convert a lay-up from the right side and will miss a good number of lay-ups taken in the middle or from the left side.

With this in mind, let's organize the defense.

The first defensive player should get into position in front of the basket about eight feet out. If he is any farther out, the offensive player can throw a short lob pass over his head to a teammate for an easy lay-up. If the defender is farther back under the basket, the ball can be brought into close shooting range before the defender starts to react.

If there is only one defender and two offensive players, the defender should wait until the player dribbling the ball gets a few feet behind the foul line and then make a rapid move toward him. This move will most likely stop the dribbler immediately. As soon as the offensive player *starts* to pick up the dribble, the defensive player stops short and backs up to protect the basket in the passing lane between O1 and O2 (Figure 10.5). This leaves the offensive player with an open 10-to-12-foot shot with your defensive player in

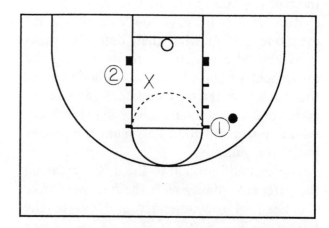

Figure 10.5. When O1 started to pick up his dribble, the defender (X) retreated to cut off the pass to O2 and get into rebounding position.

good rebounding position. That is not a bad trade-off on a two-on-one fast break. Again, the important thing is for the defensive player to make a quick move toward the dribbler, stop quickly, and back up into the passing lane so the ball can't be lobbed over his head.

If the offensive player elects to keep dribbling, the defensive player is in good position to cut off the open lane to the basket from the right side of the dribbler. If the ball handler takes one or two more dribbles, it will be difficult to lob the ball over the defender's head because all players are now only a few feet from the basket. This situation also often creates a walk or a three-second violation.

In a three-on-one situation, the defender makes the same move to check the dribbler and then backs up quickly. The dribbler is now stopped near the foul line and has a choice of two offensive players to pass to; but, again, they have now moved into a much smaller space, and the defender has a good chance of either deflecting a pass or getting into good position to guard whichever offensive player receives the pass. Reinforcements should soon arrive.

If there are two defenders, they should set up in an I formation as shown in Figure 10.6.

The first defender has the responsibility of checking the ball and, if it is a two-on-two fast break, staying with the ball handler. The second defender picks up the other offensive player.

In a three-on-two fast break, the first defender checks the ball, and the second defender remains in position waiting to see which offensive player the ball handler will choose to pass to. The second defender guards that person, arriving as soon as the pass arrives. The first defender, who started backpedaling as soon as the guard picked up his dribble, guards the third offensive player (Figure 10.7). Again, the guard who brought the ball up the court is left open for a 10-foot jump shot with both of your defenders in good rebounding position.

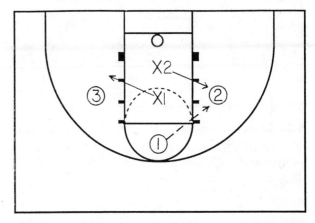

Figure 10.7. Three-on-two fast break: the first defender stops the ball, the second defender guards the first pass, and the first defender guards the second pass.

If the other team is getting fast breaks with four and five players down the court and you only have one or two defenders back, you've got a real problem. Chances are your starters are too tired and you need to put in a bunch of substitutes. In practice, go back to work on the transition game (Chapter 13).

After covering each of these situations with the team, divide them into groups of three, with each practicing the two-on-one

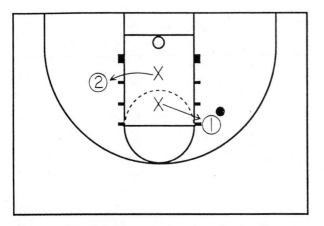

Figure 10.6. Two-on-two fast break: the first defender stops the ball and the second defender picks up the other offensive player.

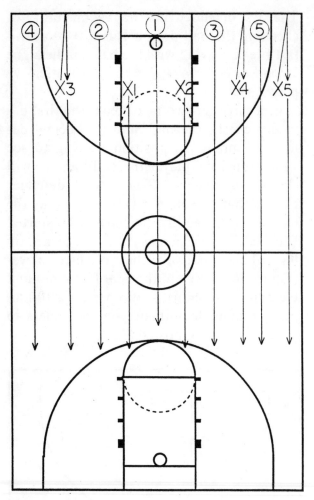

Figure 10.8. Defensive drill: X1 and X2 retreat directly while X3, X4, and X5 must first touch the baseline before retreating.

fast break at different baskets. The players can alternate at each position. Later, divide into groups of four players to practice the three-on-one in a similar fashion, and so on.

Finally, run the drill shown in Figure 10.8: with the point guard, O1, handling the ball, all five offensive players start running the length of the court. X1 and X2 retreat as well to defend. X3, X4, and X5 must touch the near baseline before retreating to the far end of the court to help with the defense.

This gets players accustomed to falling back on defense, defending against the fast break, and regrouping to pick up their defensive assignments once the fast break has

been stopped. You can vary the number of players on offense and defense.

DEFENSE AGAINST AN OUT-OF-BOUNDS PLAY

When the opposing team is going to pass the ball inbounds near your basket, your defenders must be ready to protect the basket. Most teams have a special out-of-bounds play in which they attempt to set a screen or two to free a player near the basket; a player from the middle or the side will usually cut to the basket past the screen in an attempt to get open for a short shot. In Figure 10.9, while O5 waits to pass the ball in, O1 is cutting off a double screen set by O2 and O3.

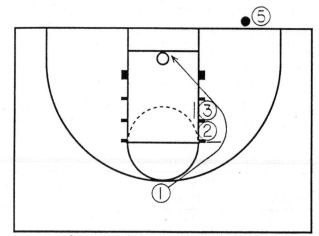

Figure 10.9. An out-of-bounds play.

I tell my players that when they are defending against out-of-bounds plays, they should not contest the inbounds pass if it is thrown out toward the three-point line. All of the players should cheat toward the middle and toward the basket, so that there will be numerous defenders in position near the basket.

To avoid screens, the defenders must stay off (away from) the offensive player unless that player is near the hoop, so that they will be harder to screen and will have the option of going above or below the screen to protect against the open pass for a lay-up. Staying off the defender is discussed below in the section entitled "Weak-Side Help."

GUARDING THE POST PLAYER

A player who receives the ball near the basket has an excellent scoring opportunity. The best way to defend against this player in a man-to-man defense is for the defender to be in a position to have an outstretched hand in the passing lane between the perimeter player and the pivot player. In Figure 10.10, defender X4 is above O4 in order to get his hand in the passing lane from O3 to O4.

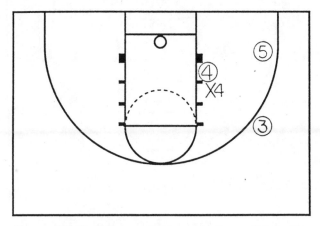

Figure 10.10. X4 can stop a pass from O3 to O4 but must reposition to stop a pass from O5 to O4.

Note that if the ball were passed by O3 to O5, the defender would no longer be in position to get a hand in the passing lane. The defender must then quickly scramble to a position on the low side behind O4 so that he can get his hand in the passing lane between O5 and O4. This can only be accomplished by hard work and constant effort.

This situation can be drilled by having two perimeter players and one post player on offense, as shown in Figure 10.10. While the perimeter players pass the ball back and forth, the defender must keep moving from one side to the other of O4 in order to maintain proper defensive position.

Another way of defending against the pivot player is to "dead-front" the pivot

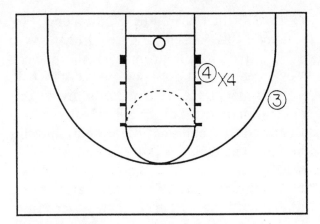

Figure 10.11. X4 is dead-fronting O4.

player. That means that X4 would be between the ball and O4 as shown in Figure 10.11. This is the most effective way of keeping the ball out of the pivot, and it is a basic element of the ball-pressure defense discussed in the next chapter. The major weakness of this position is that it is easy to lob the ball over the defender's head, giving the offensive player an open lay-up. If you wish to use the fronting defensive position, you must have strong defensive help underneath from weak-side defenders. (This concept is discussed in detail in the next section.)

WEAK-SIDE HELP

A man-to-man defense can be strengthened significantly when some defenders provide

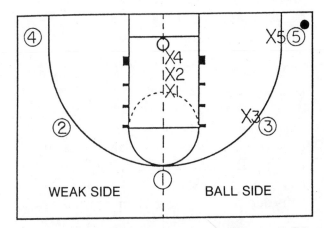

Figure 10.12. Offense is in a 1-2-2 alignment; O5 has the ball. X1, X2, and X4 have moved to help-side position.

extra help in the middle of the court. To illustrate this concept, Figure 10.12 shows a 1-2-2 offensive alignment with the players well spread out and no post player. The ball is with O5 in the corner. Let's divide the court in half and call the half where the ball is located the "ball side" of the court and the half where the ball is not located the "weak side" of the court. Defenders X2 and X4 can be much more effective if they are moved underneath the basket. In fact, X1 can also back up into the paint and help defend that area.

Note that in the area of the ball there are five defensive players and only two offensive players.

In the two illustrations given above, it is true that O5 might throw a long pass from the right to the left side of the court, for example, to O4. But there is a reasonable chance that the ball will be underthrown and intercepted or overthrown and go out of bounds. Even assuming that the ball reaches O4, the defense has plenty of time to recover. The ball is still not within shooting range, and the offense has not gained significantly by shifting the ball to the other side of the court. That statement would not be true if you were guarding a team that could shoot consistently well from long range, but that is not a problem you will face at this level of competition. To the contrary, the idea is to encourage the other team to shoot from long range because its success rate will be very low.

This principle is easily explained by categorizing offensive players as being either one pass away from the ball or more than one pass away from the ball. For example, in the offensive formation shown in Figure 10.12, (O5 has the ball), only O3 is one pass away from the ball, while O1, O2, and O4 are considered to be more than one pass away from the ball. If the formation is reset with the ball moving to O3, now players O5 and

O1 are within one pass of the ball, while O2 and O4 are more than one pass away from the ball. As the players move the ball around the circle, without defenders, they should quickly be able to tell you which offensive players are one pass from the ball and which offensive players are more than one pass away from the ball.

In Figure 10.13, the ball is with O4, but O5 has moved into the pivot position. Now O5 and O2 are one pass away from the ball, while O3 and O1 are more than one pass away from the ball.

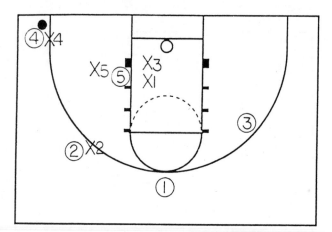

Figure 10.13. X1 and X3 are playing help-side while X5 dead-fronts the post player.

The concept of weak-side help is discussed in more detail in Chapter 11, as it is an essential element of the ball-pressure defense.

A man-to-man defense can be enhanced significantly by following these rules:

▶ When the ball is in the middle of the court the players who are not guarding the ball move somewhat toward the center of the court to protect the middle. Their arms are raised to prevent a pass into the middle.
▶ When the ball is on the far side of the court, the players on the weak side (or "help side") move into the paint (with their arms raised) deep enough so that they can watch the ball and keep an eye on

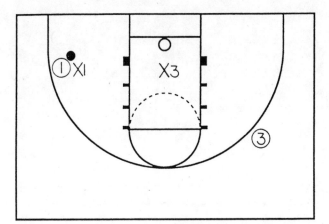

Figure 10.14. X3 plays help-side defense by moving into the paint as his offensive player O3, is far from the ball.

their offensive player; in Figure 10.14, X3 is guarding O3 and has moved toward the ball side into a position where he can see both O1 and O3.

▶ If the offensive player you are guarding moves to a position within one pass of the ball, resume your normal defensive position.

DEFENSE AGAINST SCREENS

I instruct my players never to switch on screens. Whether they go above the screen or below the screen, they still must guard the same player. If the player they are guarding does not have the ball, they should stay off the player—remain a few feet away so that they cannot be easily screened by an opponent. If they are helping from the weak side, there is a great deal of open area between them and their opponent, which makes the screen much more difficult to set successfully.

11
BALL-PRESSURE DEFENSE

In my opinion, the ball-pressure defense is significantly more effective than either a zone or a man-to-man defense at levels of play below high school varsity. The strengths of the defense are ideal to take advantage of the typical weaknesses found at the elementary and middle levels of basketball; the weaknesses of the defense are very hard to exploit by teams that do not have a high level of skill.

I recommend that a team first become experienced playing man-to-man defense; only then can ball-pressure defense be successfully introduced. I started using the ball-pressure defense a few years ago when my team had a significant number of players returning from the previous year.

A ball-pressure defense could be taught to players who didn't have man-to-man experience; but those players would be skipping a basic stage in their development, and the defense would be more likely to suffer breakdowns as well.

The ball-pressure defense has these advantages:

▶ The area of the basket is well protected.
▶ The pass into the pivot becomes very difficult.
▶ It forces poor passes, which generates turnovers and opportunities for breakaway lay-ups.

CHANNEL THE BALL TOWARD THE SIDELINE

In the ball-pressure defense you must apply constant pressure to the ball to force it out of the middle and to prevent the ball handler from having an unobstructed view of his teammates. When the ball is either in the middle of the court or moved quickly from one side to the other, many of the advantages of the defense are lost.

The person guarding the ball has the following responsibilities:

▶ Force the ball away from the middle. The defender picks up the dribbler at about the midcourt line and stays about three feet away, overplaying by about one foot. In Figure 11.1, the defender wants the ball handler to dribble to the defender's left and therefore is shutting off the right side by overplaying in that direction. The defender's left foot is drawn back somewhat, which gives the offensive player an opportunity to dribble the ball toward the right sideline. It is equally acceptable for the ball to go to the left, but, as most defensive dribblers like to go to the right, it is usually easier to channel the ball in that direction.
▶ The defender must not allow the offensive player to dribble the ball up the middle. If

Figure 11.1. The defender overplays to the dribbler's left, with an open stance, encouraging the dribbler to go right.

the offensive player can successfully do that, the defense may give up a lay-up or a relatively short jump shot.

▶ Encourage the offensive player to pick up the dribble by applying intense pressure— that is, by staying very close to the offensive player. The defender gets help from the sideline, as the offensive player runs out of room, and also from teammates (see below).

▶ Once the offensive player has picked up the dribble, the defensive player moves to within inches of the offensive player and jumps up and down waving his arms. He tries to make it as difficult as possible for the offensive player to pass the ball into the pivot or have a clear view of the court. He does not reach in to try to steal the ball, as that is likely to produce a foul.

The defender who is guarding the ball stays between the offensive player and the basket and is as close as possible to the dribbler. This is the key defensive position on your team; it is also very tiring. You will

need two guards who are able to do this; alternate them frequently during the course of the game.

ON THE LINE, UP THE LINE

When your offensive player is one pass away from the ball, the proper position to play is "on the line, up the line," as shown in Figure 11.2. The "line" is an imaginary line drawn from the offensive player with the ball to all other offensive players who are one pass away from receiving the ball. (Of course, the location of these imaginary lines changes each time the ball is passed or dribbled.)

Figure 11.2. On-the-line, up-the-line position with one hand in the passing lane.

Figure 11.3 shows the passing lanes, or lines, between O1 and O2 and between O1 and O3. In Figure 11.4, defenders X2 and X3 are in the on-the-line, up-the-line position.

"On the line" means that a player has at least some part of his body, even if it is only a hand or a foot, directly on the line. This significantly increases the chances for stealing a pass or causing the offensive player with the ball to throw a bad pass, as all possible passing lanes are closed off.

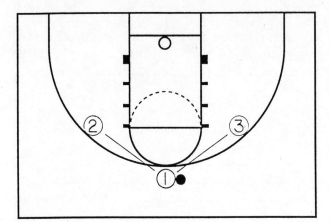

Figure 11.3. The passing lanes from O1 to O2 and O1 to O3.

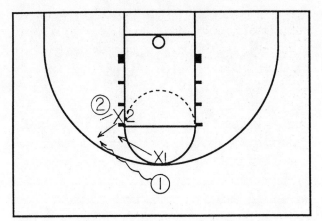

Figure 11.5. From the on-the-line, up-the-line position, X2 is able to help X1 by cutting off the dribbler, O1, ahead of the screen.

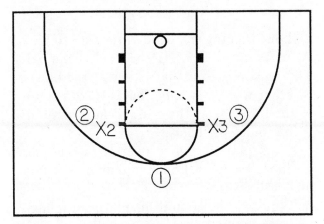

Figure 11.4. X2 and X3 are in the on-the-line, up-the-line position.

"Up the line" means that a defensive player is between the player he is guarding and the ball. This position is superior to the straight-up position of the man-to-man defense because it enables the player to get into position to deflect the pass or steal the ball. It is true that the offensive player can more easily cut to the basket to receive a pass, but don't forget that at least one and usually two extra defenders are in the area of the basket to stop the back-door cut to the hoop.

The defensive players guarding an opponent who is one pass away from the ball must also help the teammate who is guarding the ball. This help consists of cutting off the dribbler, as shown in Figure 11.5. Here X2 has temporarily left the player he is guarding

to force the ball handler to pick up the dribble. The most important part of providing help is to provide it early. That is, X2 should step in front of O1 to force him to terminate the dribble as soon as possible.

After helping, the defender must recover quickly. In Figure 11.5, as soon as X2 sees the dribbler about to stop, he immediately reverses direction to get into the on-the-line, up-the-line position. He still has the primary responsibility for guarding O2. This technique is called "early help and recovery." Again, if O2 cuts to the basket as X2 is helping, the help-side defenders can stop O2 from getting a pass near the basket.

HELP-SIDE POSITIONING

Defenders who are temporarily not needed elsewhere can help their teammates by getting into the key. If a defender's opponent is more than one pass away, the defender can play help-side defense—that is, he is available to move into the key to help defend and rebound. In Figure 11.6, X2, X4, and X5 are all guarding opponents who are more than one pass away from the ball. With X2, X4, and X5 in the paint, note that there are five defensive players against two offensive players on the ball side of the court. The defensive team is able to block the area under-

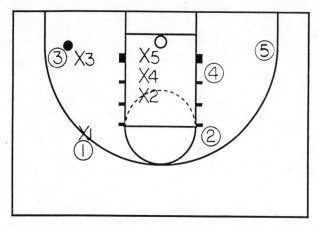

Figure 11.6. Three players, X2, X4, and X5, are in the help-side position. Note that on the ball side of the court there are five defensive players against two offensive players.

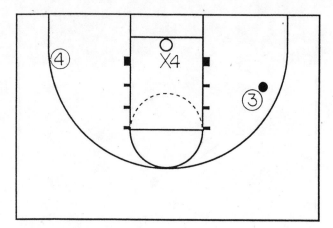

Figure 11.7. X4 is guarding O4 in the shallow-triangle position.

neath the basket entirely and is in a dominating rebounding position as well.

Help-side defenders can use this guide to position themselves on the court: the help-side defender, the player he is guarding, and the player with the ball form a shallow triangle, with the help-side defender in the paint. In Figure 11.7, for example, O3 has the ball and X4 is guarding O4, who is more than one pass away from the ball. X4 moves into the paint, forming a shallow triangle with O4 and O3.

There are two rules to determine how low (close to the basket) a defender playing shallow triangle should be. He must be able to watch both his offensive player and the ball

without turning his head from side to side. Also, he must "sink" to the level of the ball. That means he must be as low as the ball is. In other words, he must be at least as close to the baseline as the ball, without actually going under the basket.

If his player crosses over to a one-pass position, X4 can get back into an on-the-line, up-the-line position; he can also get into a ball-pressure position if his player ultimately receives the ball.

While O4 is more than one pass away from the ball, however, X4 is available to help the other defenders by getting in position close to the basket, with arms wide and held up, as shown in Figure 11.8. This posi-

Figure 11.8. Help-side position: Number 43 is in the shallow triangle with knees bent and arms up. Note that now she should be in the on-the-line, up-the-line position because player number 33 has moved to within one pass of the ball.

tion discourages passes into the pivot area and generally discourages the ball handler from either passing the ball in or dribbling the ball to the basket.

In Figure 11.8, defensive player number 43 is in the shallow-triangle position. She can see the ball and the player she is guarding—player number 33. But 33 has moved toward the basket and is now almost at the foul lane—she has moved into a position that is one pass away from the ball. Number 43 is a step or two late in moving out of the shallow triangle into the on-the-line, up-the-line position. When 33 was three or four steps back toward the sideline, 43 was in the right defensive position; but as 33 moved closer to the basket, 43 should have moved out to intercept her.

The shallow-triangle principle applies even if the opposing player is a guard. In Figure 11.9, O2 is a guard who is more than one pass away from the ball. X2 sinks to the level of the ball, in this case almost under the basket.

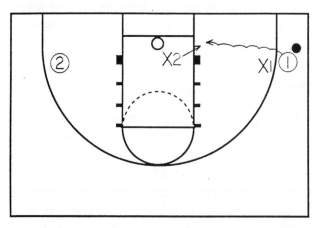

Figure 11.9. O1 drives around X1 but is stopped by X2, playing help-side defense.

A defender whose offensive player is more than one pass away from the ball has another responsibility. If there is no offensive player in the pivot area, the help-side player must "fill" the void created by the lack of the defender who would normally be guarding the opposing team's center. For example, in

Figure 11.9 X2 is playing help-side defense in proper shallow-triangle position. However, if O1 dribbles around X1, there is no defender to stop O1 from dribbling all the way to the basket. X2 must fill in this position. There will be times when a player who starts on the left side of the court, as X2 did here, actually ends up on the right side of the court in a position normally filled by the center.

The final job of the defender whose offensive player is more than one pass away from the ball is weak-side rebounding. As shown in Figure 11.10, if X4 is guarding in the

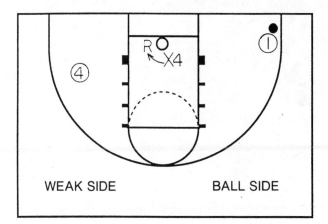

WEAK SIDE   BALL SIDE

Figure 11.10. When O1 shoots, X4, playing help-side defense, must retreat to position R.

shallow triangle, in the event that O1 shoots the ball, the most likely place where the rebound will go is shown by the letter R. O4, the offensive player guarded by X4, will likely be charging to the basket to obtain that position. As soon as the ball is shot—and this must be well drilled—X4 backs up quickly to get into rebounding position R.

PIVOT-AREA DEFENSE

When an offensive player is in position to receive a pass and make a power move to the basket, the defender should dead-front the offensive player. A defensive player in a dead-front position is between the pivot player and the other offensive player with the ball (Figure 11.11).

Figure 11.11. Number 24, the defender, dead-fronts the opposing post player to deny the entry pass.

This is a very powerful position because it shuts off any chest or bounce pass into the pivot. The only way to get the ball into the pivot, then, is a lob pass over the head of the defender to the center, right in front of the basket. That pass is shut off by the presence of the help-side defenders. The center is sandwiched between two defenders, and there is no room for the lob pass to be thrown.

Needless to say, it is vital that the help-side defense arrive. The defender guarding the pivot cannot be looking around to see if help is there; he must assume that help is there and defend by dead-fronting the pivot.

COLLAPSE TO THE MIDDLE

Every once in a while—no matter how good the defense—there will be a lapse, and the ball will get into the hands of an opposing player near the basket. In that case, it is the responsibility of all five players on the team to collapse to the offensive player who has received the ball. If that offensive player returns the ball to the outside, the defenders return to their normal position.

SCREENS

The rule for dealing with screens set by the offensive players is the same as in a man-to-man defense: never switch on screens. The defensive player retains the responsibility of guarding the same offensive player no matter where he may go on the court.

It is easier to avoid being screened out in the ball-pressure defense. Because a player in a help-side defensive position does not stand right next to the offensive player, he can move to either side of the screen to stay with the player he is guarding.

COMMUNICATION

Your defenders cannot be fully effective unless they communicate. There are a variety of situations that require defenders to talk to each other; these are discussed in Chapter 10.

DRILLS

In drilling your team, it is important to emphasize the aggressive nature of the ball-pressure defense. The players sprint back and then attack the offensive team by forcing the ball toward the sideline and by cutting off most or all of the passing opportunities. If defenders are able to do this consistently, they will not only generate a lot of turnovers but several of those turnovers should lead to uncontested baskets as they move into the passing lanes and steal the ball.

The most effective drill for learning basic positions is the shell drill, set up as shown in Figure 11.12. O5 has the ball, and the defenders get into their proper positions. If a defender is standing in the wrong position, ask either the whole team or one player to

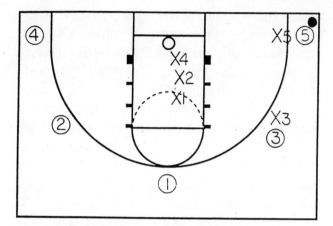

Figure 11.12. The shell drill begins: O5 has the ball; X1, X2 and X4 play help-side, X5 plays straight up, and X3 plays on the line, up the line.

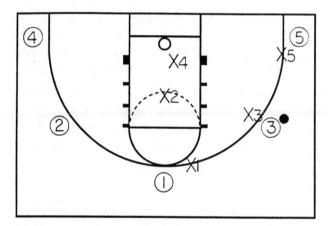

Figure 11.13. The ball moves to O3: X2 and X4 play help-side, X3 plays straight up, and X1 and X5 play on the line, up the line.

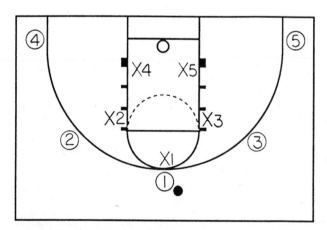

Figure 11.14. When the ball is in the middle, the ball-pressure defense is at its weakest. To protect the middle, X2 and X3 move toward the middle although their players are one pass from the ball.

tell you who is in the wrong position and what the correct position is. The ball is then passed to O3, and the players walk to their proper defensive positions (Figure 11.13). O1 is next; the proper defensive positions for that formation are shown in Figure 11.14.

When the ball has traveled completely around the circle and each defender has had an opportunity to get used to the correct position, run the drill several more times so that the players can get accustomed to the concept of the defense. This concept will be new to virtually all of your players and they are apt to feel lost for a while. Run the drill slowly at first, until the team is consistently in the correct position. Only at this point should the ball move more quickly around the perimeter.

The same drill should be repeated against a 2-1-2 offense (Figures 11.15 through 11.17). Again, each time that a defender is out of position, ask the team or one team member to state who is out of position and what the correct position should be.

Once the players have learned their general positions against a static offense, isolate each of the individual skills. All of the players should have learned basic straight-up defense so that each can guard the player with the ball appropriately. The only adjustment for ball-pressure defense when guarding the ball is an open stance to push the dribbler toward the sidelines. Next, isolate the help-and-recover situation by using a two-on-two drill as shown in Figure 11.5. In this case, X2 helps X1 force O1 to terminate the dribble and then recovers quickly to guard O2, returning to the on-the-line, up-the-line position.

The shallow triangle should be drilled with just a ball handler (O3), another offensive player (O4), and a defender (X4) (see Figure 11.7). O3 and O4 move about the court, with O4 staying on the weak side. X4 has two adjustments to make to keep proper position. He must sink to the level of the ball; that is, when O3 moves closer to the basket, X4

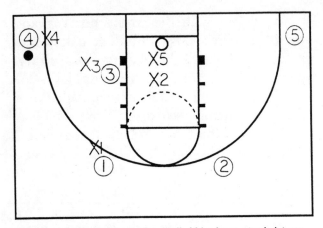

Figure 11.15. O4 has the ball: X4 plays straight up, X3 dead-fronts the post player, X1 plays on the line, up the line, and X2 and X5 play help-side.

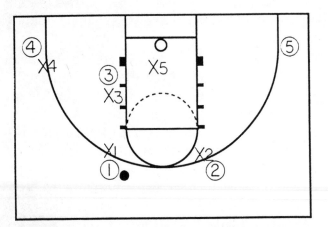

Figure 11.16. The offense has a two-guard front and O1 has the ball: X1 plays straight up, X2 and X4 play on the line, up the line, X3 dead-fronts, and X5 plays help-side.

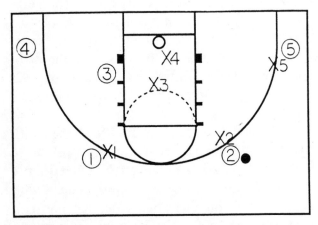

Figure 11.17. O2 has the ball: X3 and X4 play help-side, X1 and X5 play on the line, up the line, and X2 plays straight up.

must likewise get closer to the basket. Also, as O4 moves closer to the baseline, X4 must do so too, adjusting his shallow-triangle position so he can see his offensive player, O4, and the ball handler, O3.

The "fill" responsibility of the defender can be drilled by a two-on-two situation, as shown in Figure 11.9: as O1 starts to drive the baseline, X2 leaves his man and moves to help. In all of the drills above, O1 should be allowed to shoot the ball at times to be sure that X2 is getting back into proper rebounding position on the weak side.

The weak-side rebounding responsibility is drilled by isolating that situation as shown in Figure 11.10. Here, X4 is playing help-side defense and has left the defensive rebounding area temporarily. When O1 shoots the ball, X4 must scramble back quickly into rebounding position.

Drilling against screens by offensive players again involves isolating each of the typical screening situations: defenders playing in the straight-up, on-the-line, up-the-line, and help-side positions.

Finally, the individual skills are completed by having frontline players practice the dead-front position on the opposing center. That drill can be extended to bring in an additional offensive and defensive player on the weak side to practice weak-side help as well as getting into position for rebounds.

Be sure to emphasize the importance of keeping the ball out of the middle. On those occasions when the ball does get to the middle, usually near the foul line, all of the players must collapse toward the middle. This will stop a lay-up but will often leave a short open jump shot available to the offense. Players must constantly be reminded to cheat toward the middle and toward the basket when in doubt. Remind them that if they get confused and don't know what position to be in, they should head for the paint, near the basket, and then move out to the player they are guarding to get into the flow of the defense.

Now the team is ready to practice all of the skills, basically walking through various offensive maneuvers. Finally, the offense can go at full speed with the defense adjusting accordingly.

FOR MORE INFORMATION

Pressure Defense—a System, by Coach Dick Bennett of the University of Wisconsin–Green Bay, is an excellent video that provides a more complete explanation of the defense and some scenes from both practices and games. The video is available from Championship Books and Video Productions, P.O. Box 1166, ISU Station, Ames, Iowa 50010 (515) 292-7234.

12
OFFENSE

The ideal offense for beginning and intermediate levels of play should

▶ Be effective against both zone and man-to-man defenses
▶ Create scoring opportunities from close to the basket
▶ Teach basic techniques
▶ Be uncomplicated
▶ Avoid repetitious patterns

Whether you are playing against a zone or a man-to-man defense, you must create scoring opportunities from the inside. An offense that creates outside scoring opportunities usually isn't productive because of the low percentage of shots that are made from the outside; but if your team doesn't shoot at all from the outside, the defense can pack in and make scoring from inside very difficult.

You will greatly enhance the future development of your players by teaching them the basic offensive techniques of basketball—working the ball into the pivot, moving the ball from side to side against the zone, spreading the court, and so on. Complicated plays don't work with inexperienced players—there are too many opportunities for errors to occur. If your team is truly playing at a beginning level, the shot should be taken after two or three passes because a turnover

is likely to result if the ball is passed more often. You cannot expect several players to perform specific maneuvers, such as screening and cutting, with correct timing until they are more experienced. As the players become more skillful, you can incorporate offensive maneuvers that take longer to develop.

Finally, avoid spending a great deal of practice time learning one offensive pattern. There are so many fundamental techniques to learn that it is not an effective use of time to spend many practice hours learning to run offensive patterns.

I try to accomplish these objectives by using several uncomplicated ways of attacking the defense. It might be inaccurate to call them full offenses; rather than relying on all five players to execute a series of movements correctly, they rely on a few players to move the ball quickly into an effective shooting position.

For example, most offenses present multiple options. After the first pass is made, one or more screens will occur, providing opportunities to shoot or drive the ball to the basket. If those opportunities are not taken, the ball is passed to a second player, and other screens or cuts are occurring to create still more options. I feel this type of attack is too complicated for inexperienced players.

Before selecting an offense, consider players' strengths and how best to utilize those strengths. For example, if one of your players is adept at driving the ball to the basket, your offense should have a variation that clears one side of the court for that player and gets the ball in his hands. Throughout the season you should be asking yourself if your players have learned any new skills that you are not taking advantage of in your offense.

1-2-2 OFFENSE

I like the 1-2-2 formation because the passes on the perimeter tend to be shorter and thrown at a safer angle than those in a two-guard front. Figure 12.1 shows the outside three players in the 1-2-2 (the triangle); Figure 12.2 shows the two-guard front. The passes from O1 to O2 and O1 to O3 in Figure 12.1 are both short passes (the pass from O2 to O3 is not available, as defenders would be blocking that passing lane). The pass from O1 to O2 in the two-guard front (Figure 12.2) is a longer pass. Additionally, the passes in the triangle are thrown at an angle that makes them harder to steal. The passes in the two-guard front are thrown straight across the court, or at a lesser angle, and are therefore somewhat easier to steal.

Of course, by using three players on the outside, rather than two, you are giving up some rebounding strength underneath. On the other hand, you are not likely to give up lay-ups off stolen passes.

The players in the 1-2-2 are the point guard (O1), the two wings (O2 and O3), and the two forwards (O4 and O5). The 1-2-2 can be used in several ways to attack a zone with a two-man front, such as the 2-1-2 or 2-3, the most common zones. It can also be used against a man-to-man defense.

The different offensive attacks are discussed below. I give each one a name for easy reference. I try to make the name descriptive but not obvious. For example, as your team is coming down the court, you don't want the point guard to be shouting "Give and go" as the play is about to develop.

Closed

The "closed" formation is a good offense for a team with little experience; it can be put together with limited practice time. It is used only against 2-3 or 2-1-2 zones. The offense follows naturally from the footwork drills that are recommended in Chapter 4; it is also a good lead in to a more complicated offense as your team grows more experienced.

The basic position of the closed offense is shown in Figure 12.3. It matches three offen-

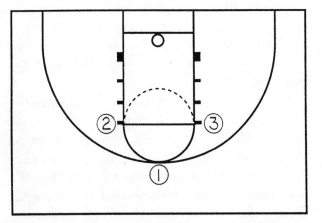

Figure 12.1. The outer triangle of the 1-2-2 offense.

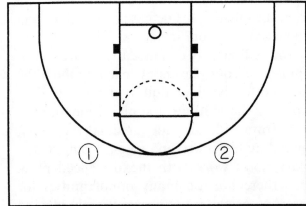

Figure 12.2. A two-guard front.

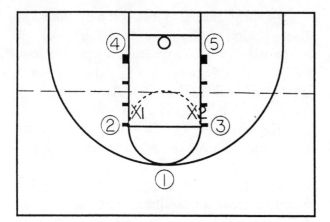

Figure 12.3. Above the dotted line, the two defenders must guard three offensive players.

sive players on the outside against two defenders: Above the line the offensive players outnumber the defensive players. Below, the defenders outnumber the offensive players.

The three perimeter players move the ball from side to side. For example, O1 initiates the offense by passing to O2, who has the option of shooting or returning the pass to O1. Again, O1 can pass to either O2 or O3.

The first advantage of this offense is that it creates open shots from just inside the foul line. The wings (O2 and O3) must be positioned to receive the ball within their effective shooting ranges.

To open the passing lanes, the wings may have to move farther from the basket. When a wing thinks he will be open for a shot, he steps up into shooting range (at the end of the foul line or lower) while the ball is being passed from the other wing to the point guard. Then, when he receives the pass from the point guard, he will be in shooting position. There won't be time to receive the ball and then take one dribble to get into shooting position.

Let's use O2 as an example, although O2 and O3 function interchangeably. O2 will normally be just outside of shooting range to afford O1 a clear passing angle. When the ball goes to the other side of the court, as in a pass from O1 to O3, O2 moves into his

shooting range to receive the pass. His left foot is the pivot foot (proper footwork is discussed in Chapter 4). He steps toward the passer with his right foot, receives the ball, pivots to face the basket, and shoots. If you have a player who can shoot three-pointers, that player simply steps back toward the three-point line for the shot.

The basic dilemma for the defense is that two players simply can't cover three players. After the ball is passed three or four times, a perimeter shot should be open. If the two defenders elect to just cover the wings, O1 can step up to the foul line for an open shot.

A second option for the wings is to drive the ball toward the baseline, as shown in Figure 12.4. The forward, O5, sets a screen for O3, who stops his dribble in a jump stop.

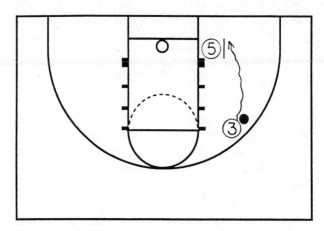

Figure 12.4. O5 screens for O3 to shoot the ball.

As he does so, he turns in the air to land square toward the basket. This creates an open 8-to-10-foot shot. The wing should not have any trouble initiating the drive because the defender will almost always be a step behind the ball as the two defenders try to cover the three players.

I usually designate one or both forwards to be offensive rebounders in the closed formation. One weakness of the zone is that as the defenders shift positions as the zone shifts from side to side, the weak-side rebounding area is left wide open. The offensive forward can slip in and out of that area and collect a lot of offensive rebounds; he is in good position because the ball will be shot from the other side, from about 8 to 12 feet out, which produces rebounds in the 45-degree weak-side rebounding area (Figure 12.5). The importance of this last aspect of the attack should not be overlooked. The perimeter players will be taking relatively good shots, and the rebounds should not be bouncing too far from the hoop. The offensive player can slip in behind the defense to collect these rebounds and have some uncontested shots at the basket.

Figure 12.5. O4 is in the best rebounding position when O3 shoots from the opposite side of the court.

Another advantage of this attack is that the players are moving the ball quickly from side to side against the zone—one of the basic ways of attacking a zone defense—and learning proper passing techniques. The offense is very easy to learn; essentially, when your team has completed the drills in Chapter 4, it has this offense in place except for emphasizing rebounding and transition assignments.

When a shot is taken, the point guard and the shooter drop back to play defense, while the two forwards and weak-side wing are offensive rebounders. If you are playing against a team that likes to fast break, O1, O2, and O3 can all fall back to protect the basket.

This formation also has some drawbacks. There is almost no motion in the offense. All of the players basically stay in place except for the forwards, who move in and out looking for offensive rebounds. An offense that has no motion is relatively easy to figure out, and the opposing coach will soon see your game plan and make some defensive adjustments.

The defensive adjustment should produce either a man-to-man defense, or a 1-3-1 or 1-2-2 zone defense. Those defenses can be attacked by the "open" formation, a modified version of the 1-2-2, or the other formations suggested below. Also, you have at least taken the defense out of its primary formation; chances are it will not be as effective playing a different style of zone.

Another disadvantage to the closed formation is that all five players are crowded into a relatively small space on the court. This makes it difficult for the wings to pass the ball in to the forwards in the pivot area. There are simply too many defenders crowded into a small area.

Essentially, this offense can be learned quickly and produces open 8-to-12-foot shots as well as some shots after offensive rebounds.

Open

The "open" formation is especially productive against a man-to-man defense. It creates open shots underneath and opportunities to drive the ball to the basket. It can also be effective against either a 3-2 zone or a zone that does not pack in near the basket but rather spreads out as far as the three-point line to guard the offensive players.

The basic open formation is shown in Figure 12.6; essentially, it is a more spread-out version of the closed formation. If the defensive zone (or man-to-man, for that matter) moves out to guard the players on the perimeter, there is adequate spacing to pass the ball to your forwards in the pivot area for

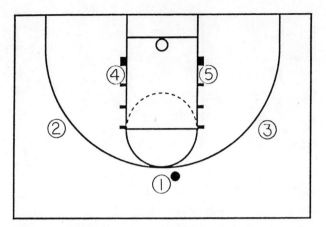

Figure 12.6. The basic position of the open offense.

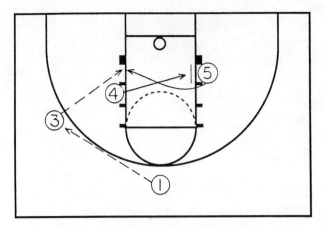

Figure 12.7. O4 and O5, the forwards, crisscross; O1 passes to O3, who passes to O5.

their power moves to the basket. The passing between O1, O2, and O3 is essentially the same: all passes go through the point guard, and the pass from O2 to O3 is not available due to the presence of defenders. The wings attempt to pass the ball in to the forwards, to drive past the defender for a lay-up or short jump shot, or to pass to one of the forwards left unguarded as a defender switches to stop their drive.

The perimeter shooters are all in position for three-point shots. If you have a good three-point shooter, you can position him, as the game progresses, in the position of O1, O2, or O3 if any of these areas are left unguarded by the zone. For example, a 2-1-2 or 2-3 zone leaves the three-point shot open from the top of the key.

This attack has some motion, in that both forwards are crisscrossing and cutting to get into position to receive a pass in the pivot area. This motion produces the best scoring opportunities.

There are several ways of positioning your forwards. If one forward is on each side of the key, they can crisscross and screen for each other, as shown in Figure 12.7. The forwards should be taught to start moving across the key when the ball is passed from the point guard to either wing. For example, when O1 passes to O3, O5 begins his cut. O3 squares to the basic position and tries to pass

the ball in to O5 for a power move to the basket.

Another way of positioning the forwards is to have the right forward be on the blocks and the left forward in the high-post position when the ball is on the right side. In this way, the wing can pass to either forward or the point guard can pass to the forward in the high-post position. In Figure 12.8, the right forward, O5, is in the low-post position, and the left forward, O4, is in the high-post position.

Many teams now use man-to-man defenses in which all players closely guard their opponents. Because the offensive players often do not have the skills to drive around the defender or to cut inside of a defender

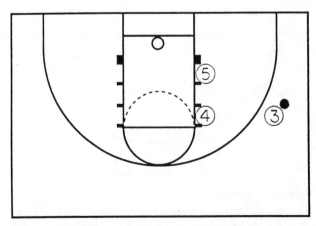

Figure 12.8. O4 and O5 are in the high-post-low-post positions.

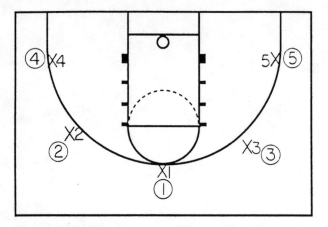

Figure 12.9. Man-to-man defense with all defenders playing straight up.

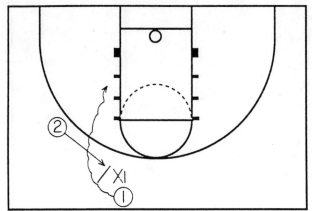

Figure 12.11. O2 screens X1 so O1 can drive to the basket.

who defends too closely, this type of defense can be very effective. The open offense offers several options to take advantage of the fact that by closely guarding each of the offensive players (Figure 12.9), the defense leaves the middle poorly protected. The middle can be attacked in these ways:

▶ The player with the ball can try to drive around his defender and take the ball to the basket or pass to a teammate. O4 or O5 can be positioned near the three-point line to receive a pass and drive to the hoop.

▶ If a teammate on either side of the ball handler can set a screen, the ball handler

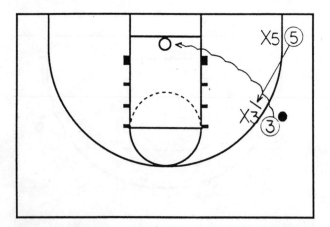

Figure 12.10. O5 screens X3 so that O3 can drive to the basket.

often will have an open path to the basket. In Figure 12.10 O5, the forward, screens for the wing, O3, who drives the ball to the hoop. The screens can be set at any point where the defender is closely guarding the point guard. For example, in Figure 12.11, the defensive player has picked up the point guard just across midcourt. O2 sets the screen to enable the point guard to drive past his defender toward the basket. Depending on the skills of your players, the point guard can pass to either forward for a spin or drop-step move, drive all the way to the basket, or jump stop and take a jump shot.

High Post

A forward can move to the high post to receive a pass from the point guard or either wing (Figure 12.12). The point guard or wings then are in a position to cut past the high post and receive a pass as they break open to the basket (Figure 12.13). Any player but the point guard can make a backdoor cut to the basket. This play is particularly effective because the defensive player (X2 in Figure 12.13) often watches the pass to the high post and neglects to watch his opponent, who can then cut to the basket unimpeded.

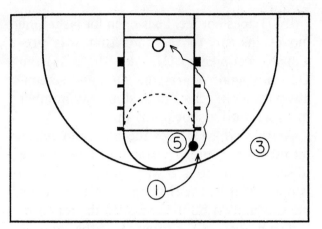

Figure 12.12. O1 passes to O4 in the high-post position.

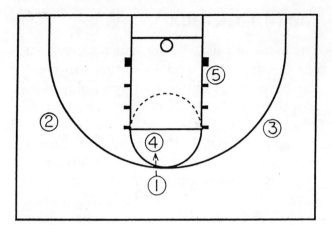

Figure 12.14. O1 cuts past O5, who gives the ball to O1, who drives to the basket.

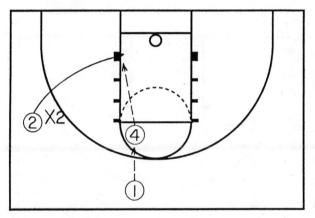

Figure 12.13. O4 passes from the high post to O2, cutting to the basket by the back-door route.

Give and Go

The give and go is very effective: The dribbler passes the ball over the head of the defender to the high post and then cuts by the defender, who almost invariably has his head turned toward the post player. The post player hands the ball back to the passer, who is cutting to the basket for a lay-up (Figure 12.14).

The same play can be used in the low-post area, with the frontline player positioned on the blocks and the passer (who is also the cutter) starting in the corner.

UP

The "up" formation, a pass-and-screen-away offense, is used against a man-to-man de-

fense. Its primary advantages are as follows:

▶ The point guard and wings have open jump shots from approximately the foul line.
▶ There are good opportunities for passing the ball in to the forwards in the pivot area.
▶ There are opportunities to score back-door baskets.

As shown in Figure 12.15, O1, the point guard, passes the ball to O2, the left wing, and then sets a screen away from the ball. O3 uses the screen to cut across the middle and receives a pass from O2; O3 turns and shoots.

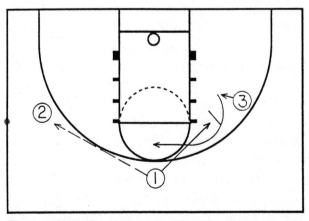

Figure 12.15. O1 passes to O2 and screens away for O3.

If O3 does not feel he is open for a shot, he moves instead to the spot that was previously occupied by O1, takes the pass from O2, and again starts the pass-and-screen-away rotation. This can be done any number of times until a shot opens up.

As the wing receives the pass and resets into the triple-threat position, he looks inside to see if a pass to a forward in the pivot area is open. If it is, the first option is to throw a pass, usually a bounce pass, to the forward.

The motion of the forwards is the same as described in the open offense. They can cut across the lane, crisscrossing and screening for each other to get open, and they can move into the high-low position. The timing is also the same: they want to establish offensive position just as the ball is arriving to the perimeter player on the same side of the court.

If the pass underneath is not available, the wing looks to return the ball to his teammate who is cutting off of the screen.

In setting the screen, the player who has just passed the ball specifically looks for the defender of the offensive player who is starting to cut to receive the pass. As shown in Figure 12.15, O1, after passing the ball to O2, cuts to his right and looks to set a screen on O2's defender.

The offensive player for whom the screen is being set, O3, first steps down and in toward the basket. If the defender does not follow, O3 can continue for a back-door basket. If the defender does follow, as will usually be the case, O3 cuts back past the screen, driving the defender into the screen.

The pass-and-screen-away offense opens scoring opportunities underneath as the forwards cross and cut into proper position. It also opens a jump shot from just inside the foul line and an occasional back-door basket. The wings can also drive straight to the baseline, jump stop, and shoot, as was discussed in the closed offense.

JACK-IN-THE-BOX

The name of this 2-1-2 formation came from one of our players who noted that the offensive player pops out of a group of players in a position to shoot, drive, or pass the ball into the pivot area.

This alignment is effective against either a man-to-man or a zone defense. It sets up in this way: Players are in a 2-3 formation, as show in Figure 12.16. O3, the "Jack," passes the ball to O1 and then runs past the screens of O4 and O5 as O1 passes to O2. As O3 arrives on the right side of the basket within shooting range—perhaps 10 feet from the

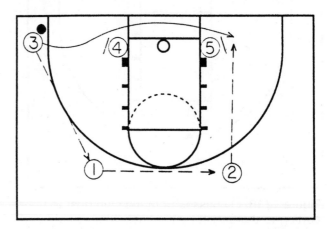

Figure 12.16. The ball is passed from O3 to O1 to O2; O3 runs the baseline and receives the pass from O2.

basket—O2 passes to O3, who should then have an open jump shot. If O3 isn't open for the jumper, the play can continue by reversing the ball: O3 passes back to O2 and heads in the other direction, looking for two more screens from O5 and O4, as the ball is reversed from O2 to O1 back to O3 on the left side of the basket.

There are two other alternatives: if the defensive player successfully covers O3 after he receives the pass, the defense has now been stretched so that a pass from O3 to O4 might well be successful. O3 could also drive the ball to the basket as a defender is running toward him. After going past the defender, he can try to take the ball all the way to the basket or, if a defender moves over to guard him, bounce a pass to O4.

If you have a player who can shoot a baseline jump shot or a three-pointer from the corner, this offense is ideal. In a man-to-man defense, the defender must successfully navigate his way through two screens to stop the offensive player from having an open shot. Against a zone defense, the offensive player is running behind the defensive forwards, who often fail to move quickly to the corner to stop the three-point shot.

Our team alternates the use of these four offensive formations during the course of the game. Even if an offense is successful, we will usually go to another formation after a while and return to it later in the game. If one particular offense is not successful at first, we might try it again later in the game as well.

FAST BREAK

The fast-break offense is discussed at the end of Chapter 13.

DRILLS

When teaching the open, closed, and up formations, divide the team into two groups— the frontline players and all others—and have them work separately on the passing, cutting, and shooting aspects of the offense. For example, in the up offense, the point and wings drill passing and screening away until they can run it well; and at another basket the forwards learn their cuts and screens. Then combine the groups to coordinate the attack. Similarly, in the open offense, isolate particular plays such as the one shown in Figure 12.4.

In teaching any offensive formation, run drills first without any defensive players on the court. Continue in this mode until players have committed the movements to their muscle memories.

At that point, add passive defense. Your players should be able to score rather easily against this passive defense. If they cannot, it could mean that the offense calls for skills that the team members do not have.

Finally, have your defensive team exert full pressure. As the team runs the offense, the defense must not be allowed to anticipate the plays and thwart them. On a give-and-go play, for example, both defenders will know what is coming since the play has been drilled repeatedly. The defenders must react each time as though they were facing a new situation.

13
TRANSITION

Transition refers to switching from offense to defense or switching from defense to offense as the ball changes possession after a basket, rebound, or turnover. Proper transition helps transform a team of beginners into a team that looks and plays like an experienced basketball team.

Speed is the key to transition. It is hard to appreciate this fact until you play against a team that can push the ball up the court quickly. If your team does not habitually sprint back on defense, the other team can set up easy baskets before your defense is prepared. On offense, if you have the time and players to install a running game, speed is also the key to success.

SWITCHING FROM DEFENSE TO OFFENSE

After a basket. The ball now belongs to your team and must be inbounded and taken the length of the court before you can set up your offense.

All of your players—particularly your inbounds passers—should be familiar with the following rules: (a) You can't throw a bounce pass inbounds that lands out of bounds first. (b) After a basket you can run from side to side out of bounds as long as you don't step on the court before inbounding the ball. (c)

In all other out-of-bounds situations, you are not allowed to run from side to side—you must stay in place and throw the ball off a fixed pivot foot. (d) You cannot hand the ball to a player who is inbounds. (e) The ball must leave your hands within five seconds—it does not have to be touched by another player on the court within any particular time limit.

I prefer to always have one starter, a forward or center, inbound the ball, no matter where it occurs on the court. This leaves both guards available to catch an inbounds pass (Figure 13.1). A second player, who should also be a starter, should get practice passing the ball in so that when your first

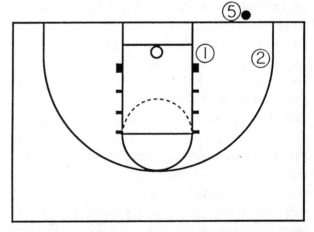

Figure 13.1. O5 can throw an inbounds pass to either O1 or O2.

player is on the bench or misses a game, you will have someone else who can do the job. Every time the primary inbounds passer leaves the game, he must tell the backup person that the inbounds passes are his responsibility from that point forward. And when the primary passer reenters the game, he must tell the other player that he will resume passing the ball in.

When you bring the ball inbounds under or near your own basket, your two guards should be the ones to receive the pass and bring the ball up the court. (If possible, give them both plenty of experience bringing the ball up the court—one guard may at times be unavailable to play.) Your frontline players should be moving quickly down the court to clear the area for the guards to receive the inbounds pass. You don't want five defenders lurking under your basket to try and intercept the pass and get an easy lay-up.

Many frontline players love to bring the ball up the court; it's usually a bad mistake to allow that to happen. The players are tempted, because they are unguarded, to dribble the ball up the court. They may very well be capable of doing that, but the problem arises when they are challenged by the defense; this is where the ball is usually turned over through a walk, a poor pass, or a defensive guard stealing the ball from behind. My standard explanation to the team on the subject goes like this: "Taller players were made to catch the ball as it falls from the sky—their job is to rebound; shorter players were made to deal with the ball near the ground, and they are the ones who are going to be dribbling the ball up the court."

After a rebound. Assuming one of your frontline players gets the rebound, he must pivot to face in the general direction of the backboard and protect the ball until a safe pass is available (Chapter 6). A rebounder who turns and faces upcourt runs the risk of immediately being tied up by one or two defenders who are still standing there. The

other frontline players should move down the court quickly, drawing their defenders with them. This prevents the defense from swarming over the rebounder and clears space for the guards.

On every rebound, the guards should retreat to the same positions so the rebounder knows where to find them—usually three or four feet from the baseline, each a few feet outside of opposite sides of the key (Figure 13.2). This gives the rebounder two possible targets. Usually the other team will not contest these passes, so it won't be necessary to have the guards move to different positions.

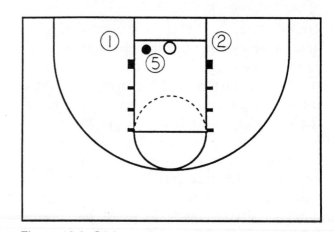

Figure 13.2. O5 has rebounded the ball; guards O1 and O2 stay back to receive a pass from O5 and bring the ball up the court.

If the other team does contest these passes, they are in a full-court press; the technique for breaking full-court presses is discussed in Chapter 14.

After passing the ball to one of the guards, the rebounder should run to the other end of the court to get into position on offense. The guards are now positioned to bring the ball up the court with one doing the dribbling and the other staying approximately even with the dribbler to afford a safety valve in the event the ball handler has trouble controlling the ball or is trapped by two defenders.

So, after a rebound, the front line is moving quickly up the court, the guards are dropping back to get the pass and bring the ball up the court. The players know where to go; the situation is organized and under control. For beginning players, this smooth transition from defense to offense is the first feel of organized team play.

DRILLS

To drill the transition from defense to offense, have five players stand on the court in defensive positions. Instruct all five players to rebound when the ball is shot. Then shoot a lay-up and have the team bring the ball down the court. To keep the drill interesting, have the guard throw a pass to one of the players for a shot at the offensive end of the court. Repeat this drill many times so that each player knows his position on the court after a basket is made. You can vary the drill by missing the shot; then the team practices the transition after a defensive rebound.

Fast break. A fast break occurs when a team switching from defense to offense tries to get a numerical advantage at its offensive end by moving the ball up the court quickly. The object is to shoot either a lay-up or any open shot before the opponent has set up its defense.

There are several advantages to a fast-break offense:

▶ Your team can score lay-ups or other easy baskets when the defenders aren't able to get down the court in time.
▶ When the other team is successfully defending against your half-court offense (the various half-court offenses are described in Chapter 12), you can change the nature of the game by using the fast break: the other team won't have time to set up their half-court defense and must defend on the run.
▶ The drills involved in practicing the fast break are excellent conditioning for your team.
▶ Your players need to learn many of these skills to bring the ball up the court suc-

cessfully against a full-court pressing defense. For example, when your forward rebounds the ball and passes it to your guard, the guard catches the ball facing the defensive basket, pivots, and drives toward the offensive basket, usually coming to a jump stop. These exact skills are necessary against a full-court press.

There are two disadvantages to the fast break:

▶ It takes valuable practice time.
▶ If your players are not skilled in handling the ball, it can create turnovers: the guard could catch the outlet pass from the forward and walk before starting to dribble; or he could dribble the ball down the court and walk instead of using the jump stop at the offensive end.

After you have installed your offense, defense, and press break you can teach a fast-break offense if time allows.

A simplified fast break begins this way: a frontline player rebounds the ball and throws the outlet pass to one of two ball handlers positioned on either side of the foul line extended. The basic configuration is shown in Figure 13.3. The frontline player (O4) who gets the rebound does not bring the ball down to chest height; rather, he keeps the ball above his head and pivots away from the basket. If the rebounder pivots toward the basket he will be much more likely to turn into a defender who can block the pass or slap the ball away.

The guard who is on the same side of the basket as the rebounder usually receives the outlet pass (O2). The other guard (O1) races downcourt about five feet from the near sideline and he cuts toward the basket at a 45-degree angle. The first forward able to do so (O3) fills the other lane by cutting in behind the guard who is dribbling the ball and running down the other sideline.

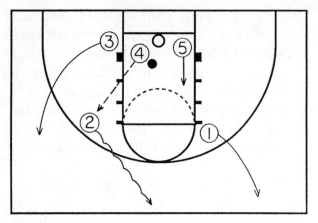

Figure 13.3. As O4 rebounds the ball, O1 and O2 move into position to receive an outlet pass; O2 receives the pass and dribbles to the middle of the court as O1 and O3 run to fill the lanes.

O2, who receives the outlet pass, dribbles upcourt quickly. He looks for the first option in the fast break: a pass to the lead guard (O1), who can drive to the basket for a lay-up or, if a defender is in position under the hoop, take a short jump shot or pass the ball to a teammate who has an open lane to the basket.

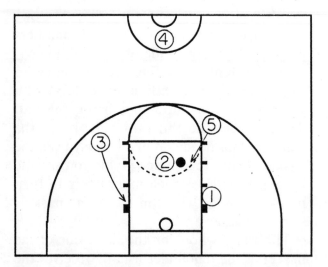

Figure 13.4. At the end of the fast break, O2 has the option of taking the ball to the basket or passing to O3, O1, or O5.

In Figure 13.4, O1, the lead guard, has stopped at the blocks as he was not open for the first option. This still leaves him in posi-

tion to receive a pass and take a lay-up or a short jump shot. O2 has the option of passing to O1 or O3 or shooting the ball himself. The other frontline players, O4 and O5, hustle downcourt as quickly as possible to get into position to rebound a missed shot or take a short jump shot from an open area. Often, one or two opponents arrive late on defense, and one of your players may be in an area of the court that is unguarded.

The footwork to execute the fast break requires the player to be able to catch the ball, pivot, drive, and jump stop. These skills are discussed in Chapters 4 and 14.

One problem your guards will frequently encounter is choosing whether to drive the ball to the basket, pass to a teammate, or pull up for a jump shot. Three choices are too many for an inexperienced player. When you start practicing these drills, first direct your players to always pass the ball to a teammate. In that way, there is no doubt or indecision in the mind of the guard who has the ball. After they are able to master this skill, direct them to always drive the ball to the basket and take a shot. Then allow them to choose between these two alternatives. Finally, work in the third alternative—the pull-up jump shot.

DRILLS

A good drill to develop these skills is called "Red light–green light": Start with players lined up at the three-point line, each with a ball, facing the basket at 45 degrees. First, simply allow the players to take lay-ups and get back in line. Then move into their path but, before they reach you, step out of the way so that they still have an open lay-up. Next, split the squad into two lines with players in one line each holding a ball. As the first players from each line run toward the basket at the same time, either allow the dribbling player to continue to the basket, in which case he shoots the lay-up, or step into a defensive position, blocking the path of the dribbler. The dribbler then must bounce-pass the ball to the other offensive player who shoots the lay-up.

The same drill can be used with three lines of players with the ball in the middle, as would be the case in a fast-break situation. This drill covers the ball handler's alternatives of driving, passing, or hitting a pull-up jump shot.

After you have drilled the basic footwork and passing techniques as discussed above, players should be ready to put these skills together in the following fast-break drill.

Players are set up in four lines—rebounders in lines 1 and 2, guards in lines 3 and 4—with one player from each of the lines on the court. Bounce the ball softly off the backboard to either side of the court. The forward who is on the same side of the basket as the ball rebounds it, holds it above his head, pivots on his outside foot, and throws the outlet pass. In Figure 13.5 O1 rebounds the ball and throws the outlet pass to O3 as O4 breaks down the open side of the court.

In Figure 13.6, O3 dribbles toward the middle of the court, O1 cuts behind him and heads down the near sideline, and O2 moves downcourt as quickly as possible.

Initially, instruct O3 to pass to O4 for a

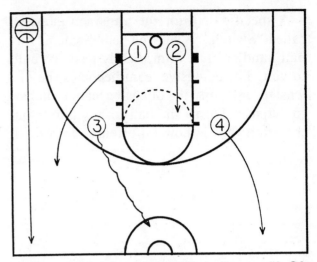

Figure 13.6. The fast-break drill continues with O3 in the middle and O1 and O4 filling the lanes.

breakaway lay-up. After drilling this skill, have O3 keep the ball and, in succeeding drills, either shoot a lay-up, pass to O4 or O1, or take a pull-up jump shot.

The drill is continuous. As the next four players step onto the court, the first four get back in line, O3 to the end of line 4 and O4 to the end of line 3. Similarly, the forwards should switch lines so that all players have the opportunity to practice these skills from both sides of the court.

SWITCHING FROM OFFENSE TO DEFENSE

A good general rule is to turn and sprint down the court immediately upon a change of possession. As players approach the three-point line, they must make sure the basket and middle are protected, that all their teammates are back, and that the ball handler's defender is in position before they move to their specific defensive assignments. Until that point, they should remain in the paint. Once it is clear that no fast break is in progress and that the dribbler has been checked by a defender, they can then fan out from the middle and guard the player they are assigned to. The player who is checking the dribbler should call out, "I've got the ball."

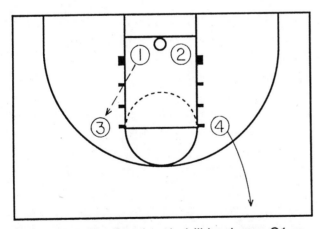

Figure 13.5. The fast-break drill begins as O1 rebounds and passes to O3, who dribbles toward the center of the court.

A specific drill for the transition game is called "Switch." When you yell "Switch," the ball handler must immediately pass the ball to you. The defensive team becomes the offensive team, and the offensive team switches to defense. Throw the ball to any player on the team that is now on offense. This drill provides opportunity for the players to get down the court quickly and get their defense organized. You can throw the ball to an offensive player for a fast break, which also gives the offense a chance to practice scoring on fast-break opportunities. It's also a good conditioning drill.

14
BREAKING THE PRESS

A good pressing defense, whether zone or man-to-man, can turn a game around very quickly. A pressing defense can induce the offensive team to panic. When that happens, passes are stolen in an area that often leads to uncontested lay-ups.

In order to avoid a panicky reaction, your players must be well drilled in their press break and be very familiar with these basic principles:

▶ Never throw a risky pass (all slow passes are risky passes) in the area around your own basket. For example, if a guard is trapped in the backcourt by defenders X1 and X2 as shown in Figure 14.1, the ten-

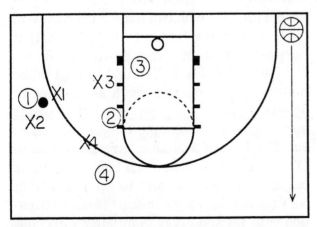

Figure 14.1. O1 is trapped by X1 and X2; the pass from O1 to O3 is too risky to throw because of the presence of X3.

dency would be to throw a pass to either O2 or O3. However, if either of those passes is stolen by X3 or X4, it could easily result in a lay-up for the other team—or even a three-point play if the shooter is fouled. I would rather have a player simply hold the ball for five seconds and lose it than throw a risky pass anywhere in the backcourt.

If the player throws the ball down the court and it goes out of bounds or is stolen by the defense, your defense will have time to get set up. Inexperienced teams turn the ball over with frequency; if you have a sound defense, your team can survive its turnovers. It can't survive giveaway baskets.

▶ Spread out. It takes two defenders to trap the player on offense who is dribbling the ball. That means there are four other offensive players and only three other defensive players. If two offensive players stand anywhere near each other, they can be guarded by one defender. That gives away your numerical advantage.

▶ Keep the ball away from the sidelines. There is more room to maneuver in the open court.

▶ Keep your passes crisp.

▶ Pass the ball before the defense can complete the trap. For example, as the offensive dribbler is being forced toward the

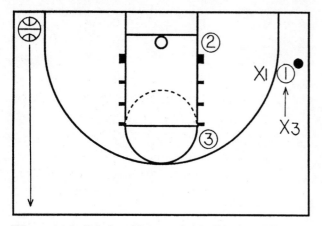

Figure 14.2. O1 should pass the ball before X3 can close the trap.

sidelines by X1 in Figure 14.2, X3 is coming up to trap. Before X3 arrives, O1 should terminate the dribble and pass the ball while he has a clear line of sight and while the passing lane is open. After X1 and X3 converge upon him, they will be blocking his vision by jumping up and down and trying to block the pass.

▶ The player who is going to receive the inbounds pass will have to pivot after catching the pass in order to face upcourt. He has to learn to catch the ball by moving toward the pass, to pivot into the triple-threat position, and to look upcourt before he starts dribbling to be sure that he doesn't charge into a defender.

Our basic position against the press is shown in Figure 14.3. This formation is intended to be used whether the defense is in a zone or man-to-man configuration. The player in the middle of the court should be good at dribbling and passing—usually the point guard (O1). The player passing the ball inbounds should be the team's best passer and the person who normally passes the ball inbounds. O2, the second guard, is on the ball side of the basket; O2 should be a good ball handler. The fourth player, O4, is at midcourt. Ideally, this player can catch a long pass, turn, and take the ball to the basket. O5 is downcourt to avoid overcrowding.

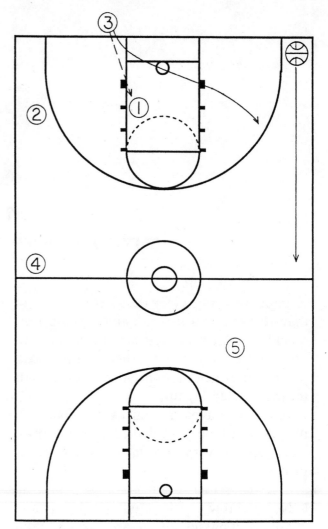

Figure 14.3. The press break starts by getting the ball to the middle of the court with the other offensive players spread out.

You may want to use a three-guard formation against the full-court press unless you have a forward who can handle the ball well.

O3 passes the ball inbounds—to O1, if possible—and moves into position as shown in Figure 14.3. The ball should be kept in the middle of the court as much as possible to avoid a player's being trapped by the sideline and to give a dribbler more room to maneuver. If O1 is not available, the pass can go to O2. If the inbounds pass is contested, these players will have to move to get free. If that isn't successful, they can start in an I formation with O4 and break in different directions to catch the inbounds pass (see Figure 14.7). If O2 or O4 catches the inbounds pass, he tries to get the ball to the point guard, O1, in the middle.

By keeping O1, O2, and O3 in a line and by passing quickly before the trap can fully close, the offense is able to work the ball quickly from one side of the court to the other to create a one-on-none or one-on-one situation and bring the ball up the court. As the defense tries to trap the ball, O4 moves around midcourt to get open for a relatively short pass—not a longer crosscourt pass. He should raise a hand to provide a target for the pass. If O4 receives the pass, he should pivot and face the basket in the triple-threat position and drive the ball to the basket or return the ball to one of the guards. Once the ball has reached midcourt, most pressing defenses will fall back and abandon the press.

The zone pressing defenses send two defensive players to trap the dribbler. This leaves the defense outnumbered four to three on the rest of the court. The zone defense solves this problem by stationing its players in the gaps between offensive players. For example, in Figure 14.4, X3 is in the gap between O2 and O3, and X4 is in the gap between O3 and O4. These defenders are trained to start moving toward the ball as soon as the ball handler picks up the dribble and then to watch the eyes of the trapped

offensive player, who almost invariably will look directly toward the teammate who is seemingly open. However, because of the trap, the offensive player doesn't have good vision and can't appreciate the fact that the defender in the gap is already moving into the passing lane to steal the ball. In Figure 14.4, defender X3 is moving into the passing lane between O1 and O2. If this pass is picked off, it often results in an uncontested lay-up for the defense.

Man-to-man defenses essentially work the same way. Once one defender leaves his man to double-team and trap the dribbler, the other defenders rotate into the gaps. Some man-to-man full-court press defenses have only one defender leave his opponent unguarded and try to double-team the dribbler and steal the ball. In Figure 14.5, for example, X1 is guarding O1, who is dribbling upcourt. X2 leaves his man open in an attempt to steal the ball while the other defenders remain in man-to-man position. Against this type of defense, only one trap can be set (X1 and X2 double-team O1); the offensive player can defeat that trap by dribbling with his head up and seeing the second defender come at him. Before the trap can close, the offensive player picks up the dribble and throws a pass over the head of the oncoming defender, X2, to the open O2.

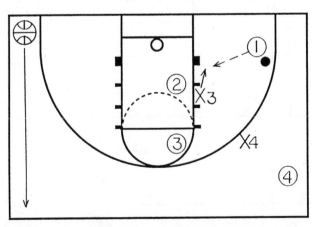

Figure 14.4. X3 is gapping the passing lanes between O1 and O2 and O1 and O3; X3 moves to steal the pass thrown by O1 to O2.

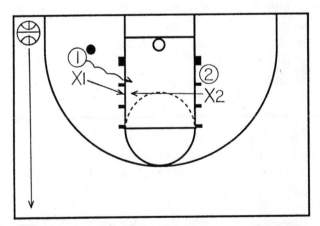

Figure 14.5. X1 and X2 seek to trap O1; O2 is left open for the pass.

Another tactic used by a man-to-man full-court press is to try to stop or steal the in-bounds pass by having each defender in the "deny" position. Instead of being between the offensive player and the basket, the defensive player stations himself between the ball and the offensive player. In Figure 14.6, X2, X3, X4, and X5 are in the deny position.

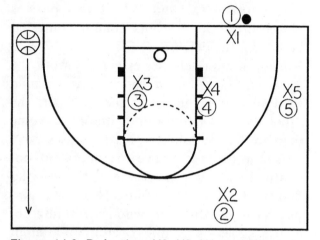

Figure 14.6. Defenders X2, X3, X4, and X5 are in the deny position, each between his man and the ball.

X1 could either guard the inbounds passer or double-team the offensive team's best dribbler. This defense is really designed to steal the ball off the inbounds pass only and is rarely good enough to set any traps after that.

There are several ways of attacking this type of pressing defense:

Quick inbounds pass. It is difficult for the defense to get organized quickly after a basket. Have the closest player to the ball grab it, run out of bounds, and throw a pass in quickly, and usually the defense will not have enough time to set up.

The I formation. Three players set up in an I (Figure 14.7); the fifth player is down-court taking one defender with him. As the I breaks, it is very difficult for a man-to-man defense to pick up the assigned offensive players.

The box. In Figure 14.8, players O1, O2, O4, and O5 form a box. O3, inbounding the

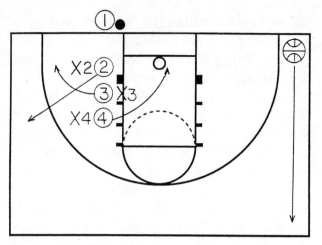

Figure 14.7. Offensive players O2, O3, and O4 break out of the I formation to open areas on the court.

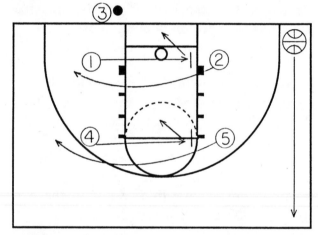

Figure 14.8. Screening across: O1 and O4 run across court to set screens for their teammates; the screeners then cut to an open area of the court.

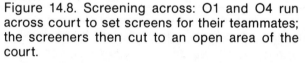
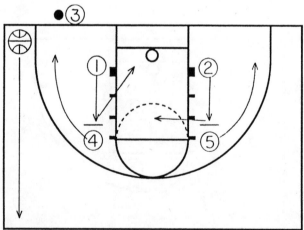

Figure 14.9. Screening up: O1 and O2 set screens for O4 and O5; O4 and O5 cut off the screens as the screeners break to an open area of the court.

ball, calls out a particular number. On odd numbers, for example, O1 and O2 cut toward each other, and one screens for the other; at the same time, O4 and O5 make the same move at the top of the box. On even numbers (Figure 14.9), the screens go in the other direction, with O1 and O2 setting screens for O4 and O5.

Baseball pass. O2 can throw a baseball pass against any defense in the deny position. The offensive player simply runs across the court diagonally with his far hand extended to indicate that he is open to receive the pass. It is also easy to set a simple screen, as shown in Figure 14.10: O4 screens for O3, who is open to catch the baseball pass. O2 can also call out a designated number for this play.

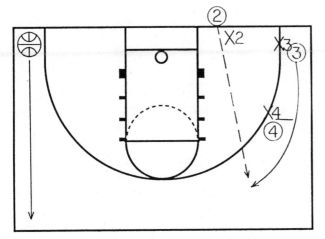

Figure 14.10. O4 screens X3; O3 catches the ball and has an open path downcourt to the basket.

Once the ball is on the court, the defense will normally fall back to reorganize in its half-court defense.

As long as the defense doesn't get good scoring opportunities off turnovers, those turnovers will not be very costly. They are offset by the fact that you will also be getting some opportunities for breakaway lay-ups against the press on those occasions when it fails. As you work on the press break in practice, emphasize to your team that no passes are to be thrown near your own basket unless the passer is sure that the receiver is open.

It really isn't practical to drill your players against every possible press you might encounter as that would be too time-consuming. We use the basic press break when the inbounds pass is not being contested. As a backup, O2 throws the baseball pass over the top of a zone or man-to-man defense that presses too tightly or tries to deny the inbounds pass. Finally, we practice the I formation break against a defense that denies the inbounds pass. We spend some time practicing this anyway, as we use this method to inbound the ball under the opposing team's basket as well.

The all-purpose drill discussed at the end of Chapter 7 is very useful practice against the press. To put more pressure on your press break, use five defenders against four offensive players.

15
PRESSING DEFENSE

After a team loses possession of the ball, it usually retreats to its own basket and gets ready to play defense. It usually does not pick up the ball until it is near or past midcourt and stays back so there are numerous defenders in the area of the basket. As shown in Figure 15.1, X1, the first defender to try to keep the ball from advancing, is picking up the dribbler, O1, just as he crosses midcourt. This style is called a half-court defense.

When a team starts its defense in the backcourt area, this is commonly referred to as a pressing defense or full-court press. Pressing defenses frequently start applying pressure at the three-quarter-court mark, half-court mark, or other locations on the court. A press produces opportunities to steal the ball and score quick baskets and can change the tempo of the game by speeding up play. There are endless varieties of pressing defenses. Also, once a pressing defense has been chosen, there are various techniques, stunts, or styles of play that can be adopted.

A pressing defense takes a lot of practice time to teach properly. In years when my team is very inexperienced, we often do not use a press at all, as I prefer to devote the practice time instead to learning basic individual and team offensive and defensive skills. When I have more experienced players, I do teach a pressing defense.

The 3-1-1 press is intended to create quick turnovers by trapping the ball once or twice in the shaded area shown in Figure 15.2. The basic alignment for the 3-1-1 press is shown in Figure 15.3. It can be used any time the other team is taking the ball out of bounds underneath its own basket. The defensive team is deployed to defend starting at the three-quarter-court mark—that is, near the foul line. This press is designed to offer one or two opportunities to steal a pass in the backcourt area while leaving ample room to retreat to a defensive position in the frontcourt when the press is broken.

The press essentially works this way: the inbounds pass is uncontested; two defenders,

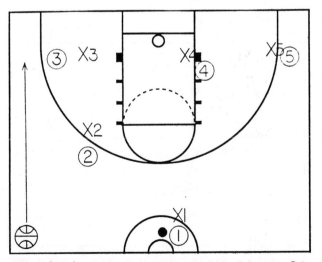

Figure 15.1. Half-court defense: X1 picks up O1 just across midcourt.

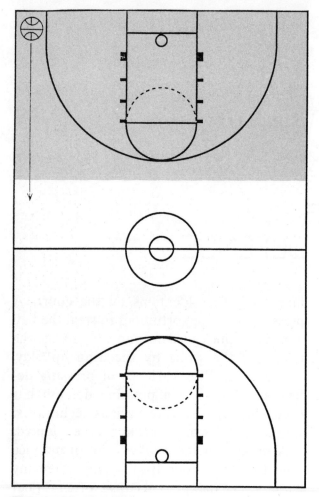

Figure 15.2. The offense seeks to trap the defense as long as the ball is in the shaded area.

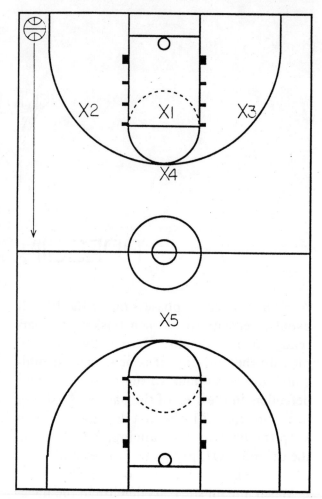

Figure 15.3. Basic position of the 3-1-1 full-court press.

X1 and X2 or X1 and X3, then trap the dribbler, forcing him to pick up his dribble. As the ball handler is being trapped, the two other defenders nearest the ball get into position to steal the anticipated pass from the dribbler to a teammate. The fifth defender may either attempt to steal a pass or stay back to protect the basket.

TRAPPING

Two defenders trap the ball handler: the first defender contains the ball handler until the second defender arrives to trap. In Figure 15.4, O1 has passed the ball inbounds to O2. X2 must prevent O2 from dribbling the ball upcourt until X1 can complete the trap. X2 allows O2 to dribble from side to side but

denies O2 the opportunity to turn the corner and head upcourt. X1 has stayed close enough to X2 so that the ball cannot be

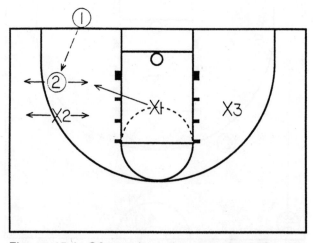

Figure 15.4. O2 receives the pass from O1; X2 contains O2 until X1 arrives to complete the trap.

dribbled between them and a few feet closer to the baseline to stop O2 from reversing field and moving to the other side of the court. X1 is now in position to close the trap at a 90-degree angle to X2 (Figure 15.5). As the trapping defenders close in on the ball, the offensive player is unable to escape. As the two defenders converge, their knees and toes are touching or practically touching. Their hands are at the same height as the ball.

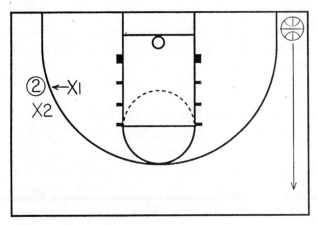

Figure 15.5. X1 moves in to complete the trap.

The offensive player is forced to pick up the dribble and attempt to pass the ball. However, the defensive players make this difficult by mirroring the height of the ball with their hands: in other words, if O2 lifts the ball high to throw a lob pass, X1 and X2 bring their hands into the air as well to try to tip the ball into the air (Figure 15.6). X1 and X2 do not reach for the ball, as this is likely to create a foul. Rather, they want to keep O2 from passing the ball for five seconds (which is a turnover), tip the pass, or at least effectively block O2's vision to prevent a good pass.

In the example above, the ball was passed inbounds on the same side of the basket as X2. Had the ball been inbounded on the same side as X3, then X3 would have the function of containing the offensive dribbler until X1 arrived to set the trap.

When the ball is passed in and the offensive player has not yet started to dribble,

Figure 15.6. Trapping the dribbler: the defender's shoes and knees almost touch at 90 degrees; their hands mirror the height of the ball.

both defenders remain about 5 to 10 feet away from the offensive player, which encourages him to start dribbling. These defenders keep their hands up and do not close on the offensive player until he begins to dribble.

TRAPPING DRILL

The basic one-on-one dribbling drill (Chapter 10) is essential to prepare defenders to stop the offensive player from turning the corner. Once your players have this skill, they are ready to practice trapping the ball.

Have three players position themselves as shown in Figure 15.7. Pass the ball in to O1. X1 and X2 must trap O1, who, of course,

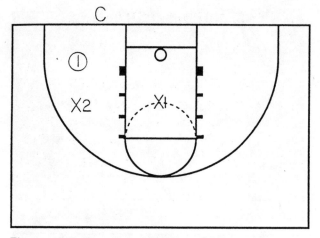

Figure 15.7. Trapping drill: X1 and X2 trap O1.

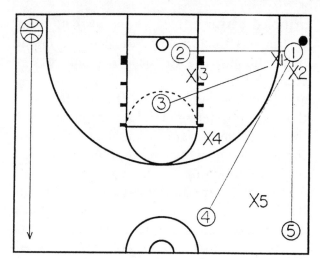

Figure 15.8. X1 and X3 trap O1; X2, X4 and X5 are gapping.

tries to escape by turning the corner and going down the sideline, splitting the two defenders, or dribbling the ball to the other side of the basket and heading downcourt. This last route is not really an escape route in a game situation: in the event that O1 succeeded in driving the ball under the basket to the other side of the court, X3 would be waiting to start the trapping procedure all over again.

After the trap is set, all three players step off the court; O1 moves to the end of the X2 line, X2 moves to the end of the X1 line, and X1 moves to the end of the O1 line.

GAPPING

When X1 and X2 trap O1, the three remaining defenders must cover the four remaining offensive players, and they do so by "gapping": standing between two passing lanes. In Figure 15.8, solid lines show the four passing lanes between the trapped ball handler (O1) and his teammates. Each of the three defenders is gapping.

Note that each gapper must get into a position to steal the ball. If the gapper is too close to the ball handler, the ball handler can throw the ball over the gapper's head. If the gapper is even with or behind an offensive player without the ball, the gapper cannot

get into position to steal the ball.

Because the offensive team will often have its players in different positions on the court, your gappers, most frequently X3 and X4, must be trained to watch where the offensive players position themselves so that they can get into proper defensive position. They should be up on the balls of their feet, keep their feet moving, and be in motion slowly toward the passer until the pass is actually thrown. This enables them to react more rapidly than if they were standing still.

Each gapper watches the eyes of the ball handler. The ball handler has limited court vision due to the presence of two defenders and wants to get rid of the ball as quickly as possible to avoid a five-second call or having the ball stolen. The ball handler almost invariably will look directly at one of his teammates before passing the ball in that direction. Because the gappers are not in the passing lane at that point, and because the vision of the ball handler is partially obscured, the ball handler usually cannot accurately see the position of the gappers. As soon as the gapper sees the ball handler look at a teammate, he immediately (without waiting for the passing motion to start) races toward the passing lane to intercept the pass.

In the event of an interception, the gapper who has stolen the ball will probably have either an uncontested lay-up or at least a two-on-one fast-break opportunity.

GAPPING DRILLS

The first drill isolates a gapping defender and two offensive players. The players are positioned as shown in Figure 15.9. O1 tries to pass the ball to either O2 or O3, who are located about two feet from each end of the foul line and must remain stationary. X1 is gapping and trying to steal the pass. The players hold their positions for five pass attempts by O1. They then rotate positions.

Emphasize the necessity for each defensive player to start in the correct position, stay up on his toes, and be moving toward the passer slowly until the passer shows the direction of the pass with his eyes. The defensive player then attempts to steal or deflect the pass.

The next drill combines trapping with anticipation. As shown in Figure 15.10, O2 tries to pass the ball to one of his two teammates but is guarded by two defenders while X3 tries to steal or deflect the pass. After attempting three of these passes, the players rotate. After each player has had an opportunity to play all three positions, the offense and defense can switch roles.

DON'T GET BEHIND THE BALL

When the ball is inbounded, all five defenders are farther downcourt than the ball is. When the ball handler has dribbled some distance upcourt before being trapped, the other defenders must react to this by staying ahead of the ball as they slide into their gapping positions. Once the ball gets ahead of the defenders, they should retreat from the press into their half-court defense. (The transition to the half-court defense is discussed at the end of this chapter.)

CHOOSING THE RIGHT PLAYERS FOR EACH DEFENSIVE POSITION

The most important physical characteristic for X1, X2, X3, and X4 is quickness. The 3-1-1 press requires players to react quickly and move quickly from point to point on the court.

X1 can be either a guard or a forward; ideally, he has both quickness and height. X1 must exercise good judgment in deciding when and where to close the trap.

X2 and X3 are essentially interchangeable and will typically be guards. The better defender will usually be in the X2 position, as that defender guards the right-handed dribblers. If the offense can only go to the

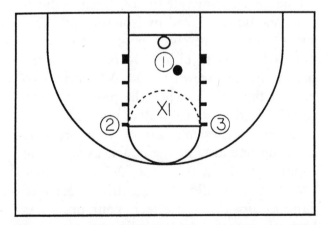

Figure 15.9. The defender, X1, gaps O2 and O3, seeking to steal the pass.

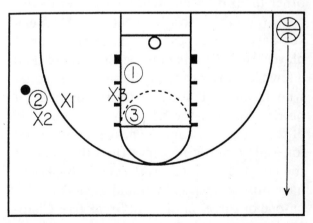

Figure 15.10. Gapping drill: X3 is gapping O1 and O3.

right side, you may be able to hide a slow player in the X3 position. If the offense has a left-handed dribbler, switch X2 and X3.

X4, typically the best athlete, has the most important responsibility: defending against the sideline pass (from O1 to O3 in Figure 15.11) and the diagonal pass toward the center of the court, passes that often lead to lay-ups or easy shots if completed. X4 is always a gapper and never a trapper. He is more in the open court and has greater distances to cover; he should be fast and have quick reactions.

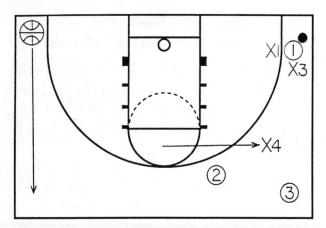

Figure 15.11. X4 moves into position to prevent the sideline pass from O1 to O3.

X5 can be a slower, less agile player, as his primary responsibility is to defend the basket. He is your last line of defense. If the other team does not send one player downcourt (and they most frequently will), X5 can act as a gapper as well if he is an agile player. However, he must never be more than a few feet closer to the ball than the defender who is farthest downcourt. In the heat of battle, it is easy for X5 to swing to one side of the court and leave the basket unprotected for a player coming down the other side of the court. It is safest to leave X5 back and have him protect as he would against a two-on-one or three-on-one fast break (see Chapter 10).

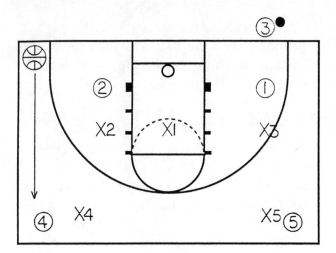

Figure 15.12. The 3-1-1 changes to a 3-2 as the offense spreads the court.

ADJUSTMENTS

Every defense leaves some area of the court unguarded. The 3-1-1 is no exception: as shown in Figure 15.3, the areas at midcourt near the sidelines are left unprotected. If the opposing coach moves players to those areas of the court (Figure 15.12), the defense must adjust by moving into a 3-2 press. However, there is one danger to be avoided when making this adjustment: you do not have a player who is clearly in the X5 position—that is, back to protect the basket. In this case, both X4 and X5 must be prepared to take the X5 position when the ball is on the other side of the court and move up to be a gapper when the ball is on their side of court. This adjustment should be drilled by isolating an offensive player who throws a baseball pass from out of bounds to either O4 or O5. As the pass is being thrown to O4, X5 retreats to protect the basket; when the pass is thrown to O5, X4 retreats to protect the basket.

Other coaches may attack your press by flooding one area of the court, as shown in Figure 15.13. In this case, X2 must move toward the middle of the court to get into gapping position. In effect, your press has now taken on a 2-1-1-1 configuration.

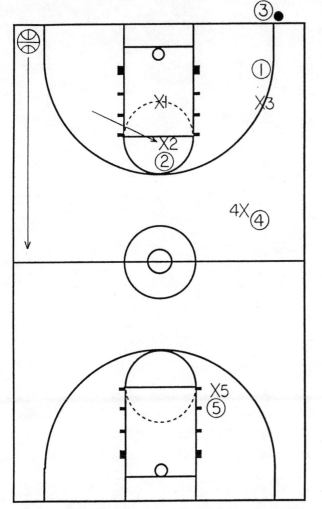

Figure 15.13. X2 moves to the middle to guard O2 as the offense changes its press break.

TRANSITION

There is no doubt that on some possessions the other team is going to break your press, which will create fast-break opportunities. Your team then has this problem: it is in a zone pressing defense and must protect the basket while it is switching into its man-to-man half-court defense.

Because protecting the basket is the primary concern, all players must immediately retreat to the paint when the press is broken. There is one exception to this rule: the defender who is closest to and ahead of the ball when the press is broken contains the ball handler and attempts to slow the progress of the offense until the defenders can get back into the paint.

Once the ball has been checked, the players then fan out and pick up their assigned opponents, again with one exception: Whoever is guarding the ball will not be able to guard his designated opponent; by the same token, there is one extra defensive player who is not guarding his opponent (the player with the ball). That player must switch his assignment to the unguarded offensive player.

The drill shown in Figure 10.8 can be used to teach an effective retreat. Vary this drill by changing the number of early attackers and defenders; for example, use only eight players on the court and have two defenders getting back early against four offensive players. Once the retreat drill has been learned, your team is ready to practice both its press break and its press at the same time.

FOR MORE INFORMATION

Basketball's Zone Presses: A Complete Coaching Guide, by Burrall Paye (West Nyack, N.Y.: Parker Publishing Co., Inc., 1983), is an excellent resource. It describes a variety of zone presses in very clear language; it also contains excellent drills.

16
THE SEASON STARTS—TRYOUTS

First, it's a good idea to recognize that each person who is trying out for your team is taking a risk—that is, risking getting cut, being told he isn't good enough to make the team. You want to be sure that everyone gets a fair tryout.

THE NUMBER OF PLAYERS ON A TEAM

I have experimented with having 14 players on a team and found that to be too many. It takes an awfully long time to do any drill when you have to run 14 players through the drill; as a result, none of the players get enough repetitions to properly learn the skill. Also, your attention gets divided too many different ways. Finally, when you have too many players, giving each of them a reasonable amount of playing time becomes nearly impossible.

I like to keep 12 players on the team, although I occasionally will go with 11 or 13. That way there will probably be 10 or more at each practice—enough for a scrimmage. Also, you will often lose a player or two during the season due to ineligibility, lack of interest, or injury.

It seems that every winter a lot of players get sick or take vacations with their parents during school term. If you don't have at least 11 or 12 players, you can really be short-handed in a game if two guards or two forwards are absent.

TYPES OF PLAYERS

During tryouts I look for two types of players: those who can already play basketball reasonably well and good athletes who may not yet have the necessary skills.

Those who play well are easy to spot in a scrimmage or as they are tested for individual skills. Good athletes who are inexperienced at basketball are more easily overlooked, as they don't have strong individual skills and tend to be confused on the court through lack of experience. I definitely look for good athletes because they tend to learn faster and ultimately play at a higher level than those with less physical ability. So, in addition to testing basketball skills, I spend an equal amount of time testing athletic skills.

Finally, I want to identify players who will either be unusually good or unusually bad at taking instructions. By that I mean that I try to identify in advance, if I can, players who will be disruptive and require a lot more time in practice than players who have good work habits. I highly value players who are willing to listen and follow instructions; they will go out on the court and do their best to accomplish what you have asked them to do.

Name	VJ	R	C	D	P	S	G1	G2	Comments

Figure 16.1. Tryout chart.

TRYOUT CHART

I use a chart to grade the players during tryouts; it is shown in Figure 16.1. The various categories are explained in the sections that follow. Find a volunteer (who isn't trying out) to help write down the scores so that you can move through the various tests more quickly.

Tests of Athletic Ability

Vertical jump (VJ). I tape a yardstick to the wall. Each player first stands on tiptoe and reaches as high as possible to see what number he can reach (Figure 16.2). The player then has two chances to jump and touch the highest number on the yardstick that he can reach. For example, let's assume that a player reaches 10 inches on the yardstick. If the player reaches 22 inches on the jump, his vertical jump is then measured at 12 inches. I record each of the marks and give the best jumper a score of 5, the next best a 4, and so on. (In my grading system, 5 points is highest and 1 point is lowest.)

Running (R). I divide the players into two groups and have them run sprints the length of the court after giving them a chance to warm up. I divide them randomly at first; then, based on speed after each heat of five players, I put them into either group 1 (slowest), group 2 (average), or group 3 (fastest). In the finals, I run the slowest group first and grade those players from 1 to 3 depending on how they finish. I grade the second group from 2 to 4, and the third group from 3 to 5.

Eye-hand coordination (C). I throw a nerf basketball to each player at different speeds and different heights from relatively close range. They have to catch the ball and return it to me as quickly as possible. The point isn't to make them run far for the ball but rather to jump, bend, or react very quickly when the ball is thrown from only a few feet away. Again, I subjectively score the players from 1 to 5. I sometimes will have the players stand about seven or eight feet from the wall

Figure 16.2. Getting ready to measure vertical jump: the player stands on tiptoes and reaches as high as he can.

and see how many passes they can throw off the wall and catch in a 30-second period.

Tests of Basketball Skills

I also grade each of these skills on a five-point scale:

Dribbling (D). I have the player dribble the length of the court and back again, first right-handed and then left-handed. I tell each player to dribble under control at the fastest speed that is comfortable.

Passing (P). I have three players set up in a triangle and pass the ball to each other; this is another opportunity to see the players throw and catch, which measures their athletic skills as well as their technical skills.

Shooting (S). I have each player take four shots from various positions on the court. I am primarily interested in observing their shooting form.

Three-on-three game (G1). I try to divide the teams so that each team has at least one guard who is able to handle the ball and another two players who are at least roughly physically matched with their opponents. Half-court three-on-three is particularly difficult to play without good basketball fundamentals. It tells me a lot about how players adapt to a new situation, their basketball skills, and their concentration.

Five-on-five scrimmage (G2). I will often join in this scrimmage, as I see a lot of different things when I am in the middle of the action.

CHOOSING THE SQUAD

It usually takes me three days to complete this process, although by the end of the first day I have made up a list of players who are certain to make the team and players who have very little chance to make the team.

I would much rather have players certain to make the team working on some productive drills during the rest of the tryouts, although I have not yet told them that they have made the squad. At the beginning of the second day I might take 10 or 15 minutes to introduce a drill to this group and have them work on this drill while I continue to test the others.

In the last stages of the tryout I will try to isolate the last six or eight players who are "on the bubble"—who may or may not make the team—and have them scrimmage three-on-three or four-on-four.

When I select the team I don't simply add up the points and see which 12 have the highest total. I use the chart as a guideline, giving some areas—such as scores earned during scrimmages—greater weight than other areas. For example, there are some players who seem always to be around the ball, and that doesn't necessarily show up as a dribbling, shooting, passing, running, throwing, or jumping skill. Yet this aggressive type of player often makes significant contributions to the team.

Be sure to balance your team with the number of backcourt and frontcourt players that you need. If you expect to be using a starting lineup of two guards and three frontline players, I would suggest having five backcourt and seven frontcourt players on the team. You may want to have six of each if you feel that you frequently will use three guards on the court.

I occasionally make more than one cut, although I don't like to do it that way. Making more than one cut unfairly singles out those who "couldn't even make the first cut."

By the end of the third day I post a list of those who have made the team; I also may speak directly to those who have not made the team and thank them for trying out.

I try to conclude the selection process in three days, but often that is not possible because other players show up late due to illness or participation in fall sports. I tell the players involved in fall sports that they are welcome to try out for basketball even though their seasons haven't ended. I ask them to come to at least one day of tryouts and assure them and their coaches that I'm not going to exhaust them during my tryouts at a time when they are engaged in the most important part of their season. And I explain that if they make the team, they can join the other players after their current season has ended.

Very often, the top athletes in the school will be playing more than one sport, and you will have to wait a week or two to get them out for practice.

17
ORGANIZING PRACTICES AND SETTING PRIORITIES

You must make the players aware of the importance of attending practices. It is easy to visualize teaching skills in sequence, but often players don't realize that when they miss a few practices they will have difficulty keeping up with the rest of the team.

Team morale also is affected when some players miss practice frequently. Those who come regularly are very conscious of how much playing time each player is getting. If a player is not coming to practice regularly or is not working hard at practice but is getting a lot of playing time, team morale will suffer.

For those reasons, it is important to have clear rules about practices. Mine are as follows:

▶ Each player is expected to come to practice every day.
▶ If a player cannot come for some reason, unless it is an emergency, it should be cleared with the coach beforehand.
▶ If a player cannot come because of an emergency, he should contact the coach as soon as possible to explain the problem.
▶ If a player is still not coming to practices, I will warn and speak with parents. If that doesn't work, I will probably have the player leave the team.

Many coaches have a rule that a player who misses a certain number of practices or a practice before a game cannot play in the game. My feeling is that a player who is a chronic problem should not be on the team. I don't like to discipline players by limiting their playing time, although I have done so on occasion.

Each week, I give players a copy of our practice schedule for that week. This eliminates a lot of confusion with players forgetting what time practice is or missing a practice and not knowing what time the practice will be the next day. Players also have a roster with the other players' telephone numbers and my telephone number. If a player misses a practice or doesn't know when a practice is, it is his responsibility to contact me or a teammate to find out when the next practice is.

I emphasize the importance of getting to practice on time so we don't lose fifteen or twenty minutes before everybody is dressed and ready. If a player is late more than once or twice, I have that player take some laps. If many players are late, I will have the whole team run some laps. However, I don't like to use running as a punishment because it is so necessary to conditioning. I am still looking for a better solution to that problem.

DIVISION OF PRACTICE TIME

In the division of time that follows, I am assuming that you have the whole gym to yourself for the entire practice. Most teams don't have this luxury and have to share all or part of their gym time with other teams; that calls for significant adjustments in how you schedule your time.

Warm up. During the warm-up period, about 10 minutes, I give the players a list of skills to practice. For example, I might have the guards do a hundred dribbles with each hand and then take 10 driving lay-ups from each side of the basket. The frontline players might practice the particular move that they were working on, such as the drop step, 10 from each side of the basket, followed by a rebounding drill.

First drill. I tend to make the first drill a very active one because the players have been sitting in school all day and aren't really ready to stand still and listen. The drill should involve full-court running, such as the three-man weave.

First teaching time. About 25 or 30 minutes into the practice, when the players are tired of running, I do the primary teaching for the day. It usually takes 30 to 40 minutes to explain the principle being taught and incorporate it into a drill.

This drill is followed by a water and rest break of about five minutes.

Follow-up drill. This drill follows up yesterday's main drill to help the players learn the skill through repetition. It usually takes 10 minutes.

Team meeting. We now meet for a few minutes and discuss matters such as arranging transportation, issuing uniforms, and paperwork. I usually take a couple of minutes at this point to explain one basketball rule each day. For example, the first day I go over the boundaries of the court and illustrate when the ball is in bounds and out of bounds. At the first practice after a game, we use the team meeting to discuss that game;

the feedback from the players is often helpful.

Scrimmage. Scrimmages give your players valuable experience and an opportunity to put the individual and team skills that they have learned into practice. The players always enjoy playing and benefit from the conditioning.

I will often set up special rules to facilitate putting into practice the skills that players have been learning. For example, if they have been working on driving to the basket, the defense is not allowed to offer any resistance if an offensive player attempts a drive.

Final few minutes. If time allows, I like to have the players either shoot 10 foul shots or make 10 foul shots before they leave.

The total time for practice is usually between an hour and forty-five minutes and two hours. I don't feel that I ought to go longer than two hours; many of my players are freshmen who are trying to adjust to high school. Also, there is a point of diminishing returns when players are tired and no longer really working productively on the court. Besides, it's important that sports be kept in perspective. Two hours a day (plus transportation time) is plenty to devote to basketball. Most seasons I cut practice time to one and a half hours about halfway through the season or give the players one free day each week.

SELECTION OF DRILLS

In many drills, all except two or three players are standing around watching. When this happens, opportunities are being wasted in two respects: the players could be practicing the skills they are working on, and they tend to get bored and lose concentration. I try to select drills that keep all of the players involved.

It is often a good idea to break the team into two squads—backcourt players and frontcourt players, for example. The guards can practice their dribbling while you work with the forwards on the drop-step move. Then, while the forwards do 10 drop-step moves from each side, you can work with the guards. I appoint two players, usually sophomores whom I expect will be starters, as team captains. I have them run drills with part of the team when I am working with the rest of the team. Of course, as very few coaches have the luxury of an assistant, you do have to pause from time to time to be sure that the group you're not working with is attending to business.

Don't select drills that take too long to learn. You never have enough practice time to accomplish teaching your players the basic skills. Drills that are very complicated to execute result in a lot of down time—that is, time when your players are not actually practicing but rather are trying to memorize the routine of a drill. That time could be better spent doing simpler drills. If you make up your own drills, be sure that you know what each player should be doing throughout the entire drill. Don't get yourself into a situation where you are standing in the middle of the court trying to figure out what happens next while your latest brainstorm turns into complete confusion on the court.

Another problem is that your players will have vastly different abilities. If you repeat every drill until each player gets it perfectly, you'll still be doing your Day 1 drills by the time the first game rolls around. I insist that at least most of the players can do a drill properly before moving on.

When you divide your squad into two teams for scrimmages or drills, you are faced with a choice of keeping your starters together as a unit or placing some starters on each team. If your starters always play together as a unit your scrimmages will turn into dispiriting routs, as the team of substitutes will not be able to compete effectively. The same thing will happen in your drills. This tends to diminish the quality of the scrimmage and lowers team morale. On the other hand, your starters need to be able to

work together effectively in order to play as a cohesive unit during the game.

I try to resolve this situation by playing the starters together about half of the time in drills and scrimmages. Often, I will start the scrimmage with the starters on one team and the nonstarters on the other team. Then, as I bring in substitutes, I will switch some of the starters to the other team so that the squads are more equally balanced.

SUBSTITUTES

It's very difficult for players to sit on the bench; they're just dying to get into the game, whether they say so or not. On youth basketball teams, very often players are assured a certain amount of playing time, so playing time does not become a major issue. However, in high school, playing time is usually based upon a merit system rather than an attempt to achieve equality.

For example, most coaches have a regular starting five and only use about three other players when the outcome of the game is still in doubt. Through this system, the starting five become accustomed to playing as a unit, which strengthens their overall performance. The timing of the offense improves as the regulars get used to receiving passes from each other, setting screens for each other, and generally knowing where their teammates are likely to be on the court at any particular time. The same holds true for defense, as the players learn to communicate with each other, handle screens effectively, and cover fast breaks.

The team is somewhat less effective with the first few substitutes but doesn't lose too much cohesiveness when only one or at most two substitutes are in the game at the same time. Unfortunately, this leaves the remaining players with little playing time while the game is on the line. Players find this disappointment hard to accept, and coaches should expect some negative reaction from the players and their parents.

To make the best of this situation, take an active role in discussing it with your substitutes. For example, at the conclusion of tryouts, I usually tell two or three players who are at the bottom of my list that I am ready to select them for the team but that I want to discuss their probable playing time. (I emphasize the word *probable* because often I have had players who improved very rapidly and earned more playing time or even starting positions.) I tell these players that it is unlikely that they will be playing much and that they're likely to find that situation to be frustrating. I emphasize the positive contributions they can make to the team. I then give them an opportunity to decide whether they want to be on the team under those circumstances.

As the season progresses, continue to encourage your substitutes. Explain to them their roles on the team. For example, you may emphasize how a particular player is contributing to the overall strength of the team with strong defense or rebounding. Each player has some strength that does contribute to the team effort. Remind them that in high school, entering freshmen often get less playing time than the sophomores who have had a year's experience in your program. This explanation can help put the lack of playing time in a better perspective.

Finally, give your substitutes as much playing time as possible. They are coming to practices, working hard, and very much want to contribute to the team effort. Get them into the game whenever you can.

Even with good communication between coach and players, a few of the players may get the impression that you don't value them highly as players because they rarely get onto the court when the game is on the line. Unfortunately, these players will also feel that you don't value them as people as well. They may have been starters or even outstanding players in earlier grades; for some it is a harsh realization that they are not being counted among the best players on the team.

In this case, you must keep trying to communicate to these players that they are important to the team as players and as individuals. You should also point out to them that it is not that they play poorly but that there are players ahead of them who have the particular combination of skills on the court that the team needs in close games.

As an alternative, you can also choose to adopt a system of giving all of the players substantial playing time when the game is on the line. The advantages to this system are that you will have fewer disgruntled players and better team spirit. Also, a greater number of your players will improve at least somewhat. The disadvantages are that your team will not play as well, as no five or six players become accustomed to playing together, and your best players will not develop as quickly. As a result, your team is likely to win fewer games. The players eventually will have to face the harsh reality of differences in ability—certainly when they try out for the varsity team.

SETTING PRIORITIES: A WEEK-BY-WEEK SCHEDULE OF PRACTICES

In setting priorities, you must perform this balancing act: each of the skills must be taught properly; but your first game is about four weeks away, and you must prepare the team to go out and play at least reasonably well.

It is tempting to think that once you explain a skill and drill it once or twice, the players have learned it and it is time to move on. Often coaches will succumb to the pressure of getting ready for the first game by jumping from one skill to another too quickly; the result is that the players don't learn to do anything right. I think that it is more important for them to learn the skills properly than it is to be fully ready for the first game. To accommodate the need to be at least reasonably ready within four weeks,

I postpone teaching certain skills until the fifth or sixth week of the season or later.

Here is a suggested practice schedule:

The first two weeks. I start off with footwork because that is essential to passing, shooting, and dribbling. I quickly bring in passing instruction, as that serves to further drill footwork.

By Day 3 or 4, I am starting players on shooting and dribbling sequences. I then add rebounding and basic defensive positions.

This rounds out the basic teaching that I hope to accomplish during the first two weeks. I don't mean to suggest that the players will have mastered all these skills within two weeks, but they should have a good start on the sequences involved.

At the same time, we do conditioning drills, scrimmage, and hold some team meetings. In the team discussions, I talk about the importance of team play and aggressiveness.

During the scrimmages, I have the players in a man-to-man defense. I spend a little time the first day showing them the defensive position of keeping between your man and the basket with your back to the basket and simply have them work on that during the first two weeks of scrimmages. On offense, I have them in the 1-2-2 configuration that they are using during passing drills. This enables them to work on their footwork and passing. The players may become somewhat impatient for you to tell them what to do on offense, but that will come later. As long as they are working on footwork and passing on offense, basic position and defense, and getting conditioning as well, the scrimmages are beneficial.

The third week. The third week is primarily devoted to team defense. Each new aspect that is introduced becomes part of what is expected of the players in the scrimmage.

During warm-ups, players work on dribbling and shooting sequences, do conditioning drills, and practice the drop-step move. Guards are added to the drills for the drop-step and spin moves (see Chapter 9).

The fourth week. If all works well, we are ready to start working against the press and begin our team offense, although I really don't expect my team to have a well-organized offense during the first game or two.

We see a full-court press in at least half of our games. Because the full-court press can be devastatingly effective against a team that is not properly organized, I spend portions of at least three practices before the first game working on breaking the press.

Everyone must be ready for the situations that arise in a game that don't normally come up in your practices. For that reason, our team plays a simulated game a few days before the first game of the season. This gives me an opportunity to run through a number of situations:

▶ The center jump to start the game
▶ Substitutes checking into the game at the scorer's table and kneeling until the referee waves them into the game
▶ Players going out and players coming in exchanging information about defensive assignments
▶ Shooting foul shots
▶ Time-out procedures

The fifth week through the rest of the season. Once your team starts playing its schedule of games, it becomes more difficult to teach new skills. Because your team is competing, the number of practices is often reduced from five to three per week. You spend part of your practice time discussing the last game and preparing for the next game, which also limits teaching time.

During the fifth week and thereafter, I have the players work on ball-pressure defense and offense and continue their sequences on offensive skills. As soon as time allows, I start working on driving the ball to the basket.

At some point in the season I will feel that our team is pretty solid both offensively and defensively. At that point, I will try to start working on a full-court press or a fast-break offense.

Most teams that we play have a full-court press ready for their opening game. I acknowledge that the press is an extremely effective weapon but strongly believe that it takes too much time away from drilling the fundamentals. If we are able to break the press—and we almost always are—the other team is usually fairly easy to beat.

Our team plays in a league with six other teams, and we play each team in the league twice. I try to introduce a full-court press or fast break by the time we start the second half of our league season. This gives opposing teams a new problem to cope with.

During games I jot down weaknesses in our offense and defense. Throughout the season, I spend a lot of practice time strengthening these areas. For example, it takes a team a long time to successfully coordinate passing the ball from the perimeter to the pivot player: it involves proper spacing and positioning of the players, proper timing of the passes, and taking the ball to the basket. By the same token, we need to constantly teach and reinforce the principles of our ball-pressure defense, such as early help and recovery (Chapter 11). There is never enough practice time to accomplish everything that needs to be done; however, the team should be constantly refining its skills and improving the level of its play as each of the component skills is strengthened.

CONDITIONING DRILLS

Here are some conditioning drills that also emphasize other skills such as concentration and ball handling:

Three-man weave. The team is in three lines (Figure 17.1); each of the players in O1's line has a ball. The drill has one basic movement: after passing the ball, the passer cuts behind the player who receives the ball and comes back around to catch a pass in

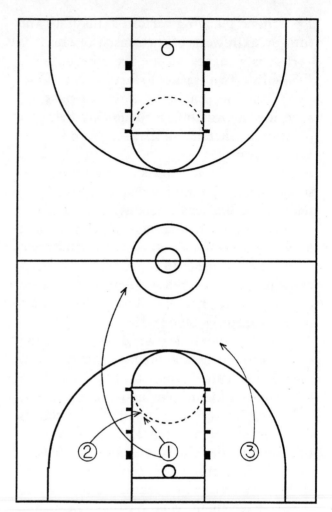

Figure 17.1. O1 passes to O2, who is moving toward the middle, and cuts behind O2. The pattern is repeated as O2 passes to O3, who is moving toward the middle, and cuts behind O3.

turn. O1 passes to O2 and runs behind O2. O2 passes to O3 and cuts behind O3. O3 passes back to O1. The passing ends with a lay-up by whichever player has the ball last. The players then form three lines, rotating to different positions, and wait at the far end of the court.

Guard and wings. This is run out of the same formation as the three-man weave. In this case, the players in the middle line are all guards. The two wings, O2 and O3, run about five feet in from the sidelines straight down the court, even with O1, the guard. O1 passes to O2, who passes back to O1; O1 passes to O3, who passes back to O1. As

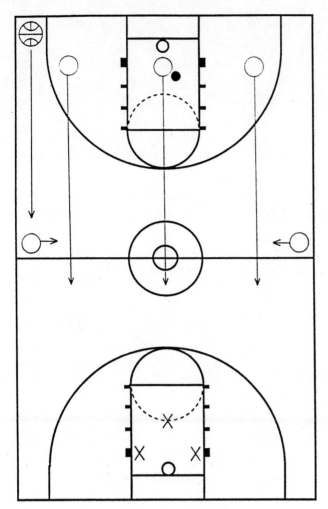

Figure 17.2. A three-man continuous drill.

soon as O1 crosses midcourt, he dribbles to the foul line, where he jump stops and passes to either O2 or O3, who have run straight down the court to a 45-degree angle from the basket and then cut directly to the basket without changing speed.

Three-man continuous drill. Three offensive players bring the ball up the court, where three defenders are waiting. There are two lines of players waiting on the sidelines at midcourt (Figure 17.2). As the three offensive players go by, one player on each sideline steps onto the court. Each defender must quickly move to guard an offensive player. The offense tries to get a good shot quickly by driving, screening, and passing. As soon as a shot is taken (only defenders can rebound), the defensive player who rebounds the ball becomes an offensive player along with the two players who have entered at midcourt; the offensive players become defenders. The rebounder passes to midcourt on one side or the other while the defenders spring back to try to stop the attack. The defensive players who walked off the court each get in line at midcourt.

18
GAME-DAY COACHING

PREGAME PREPARATION

Be sure that the correct names and numbers of all of your players are written in the official scorebook. A uniform number that does not match what is in the scorebook can lead to a technical foul. Players will sometimes forget their jerseys and have to borrow one. Keep an extra road uniform in your bag; you'll surely need it.

I expect players to be dressed and ready to play about 45 minutes before the game. The players then shoot around—my only instructions to them are to be sure to take at least two foul shots and try all of the shots they expect to try in the game. This helps them get used to the different features in each gym, such as glass or wooden backboards, wooden or rubber floors, and so on.

Half an hour before game time we review the game plan. In a practice prior to the game I will often give a few or all of the players specific goals to accomplish, such as a pivot player trying a new move or a guard driving the ball all the way to the basket. Just before the game, I talk about the basic strategy we are going to employ against the other team and remind them of their individual goals.

Before the first game, I tell the players that it is perfectly natural to feel nervous and not to be concerned about it. I also tell them that

if they are feeling especially nervous, the first time the ball comes to them they should be very careful to watch it all the way into their hands, feel it, bounce it once, and pass it back; that usually helps to calm a player down.

After briefly going through the points I want to emphasize on defense (getting back quickly, checking the ball early as it comes up the court, helping out your teammates) and offense (keep the spacing on the floor the way we did it in practice, look for a shot close to the basket, shoot when you get a good shot), I turn to any special instructions I might have. For example, when I notice a player on the other team who looks strong, I tell my player who will be guarding that player to watch her opponent warm up. This is a good way to find out if a player favors the right side, for example, or if she looks like a threat to shoot from the outside.

After I discuss strategy, the team runs through our standard pregame procedure: a team cheer as they run out onto the court, circle the court, and start into a warm-up drill. The players are then free to shoot around and do other warm-ups. For example, a lot of players will do stretches, practice passing the ball, work on a particular shot, or just generally loosen up.

I call the team in with about a minute to

go to get ready for the start of the game. I have been spending the warm-up period watching the other team. I note from the scorebook who their five starters will be and watch them during the warm-ups. I assign an appropriate defensive player to each based on position and ability.

GAME TIME

Time-outs. I consider each time-out to be a very important asset. The basic purpose for time-outs is to stop the other team when it is on a scoring run. At the JV level, four quick points is a very serious problem, and six points can be a catastrophe. I will usually call a time-out if four quick points are scored and always call a time-out if six points are scored. Usually at that point the players need to be reorganized and calmed down.

I rarely call a time-out at the end of the game to set up an offensive play because I feel that gives the other coach too much of an advantage to set his defense for the particular situation. For example, if you are three points behind, the coach may be telling his players to foul your player intentionally so you can't get a three-point play or putting his players beyond the three-point line where they can be much more effective defensively.

During a time-out I expect the five players who are in the game to either sit on chairs or stand, as they prefer, with the rest of the team gathered around, so that I can make the necessary adjustments in the team's performance. The players need to be listening and not talking at this point. Before the end of the time-out, I listen to anything they have to say if time permits.

Substitutions. Perhaps the greatest disadvantage of the man-to-man defense is that the players must constantly keep track of whom they are guarding during the substitutions for your own team and substitutions for the other team. When a number of opponents come into the game at the same time, the first defensive player to notice calls out

"Match up" and each player then quickly moves to the side of the player she will be guarding. Any confusion can be quickly resolved in that way because one player will be standing open and one player will be guarded by two defenders. All this happens before the ball is passed in so adjustments can be made.

Your players need to practice the proper response if they do not know which opponent they are guarding: Retreat to the paint, about six or seven feet below the foul line. That gives them the opportunity to protect the basket until they see which opponent is not being guarded. That opponent may be open for a 10-to-12-foot jump shot for a short time but will not have an opportunity to make an uncontested lay-up. The players soon learn that it isn't as important who they guard as it is to guard someone; it's easy to switch defensive assignments the next time down the court if a mismatch occurs.

Halftime. I like to look at the scorebook for a minute or two before talking to the players at the halftime. An opponent may have scored two or more baskets and I will not have noticed. At beginning levels of basketball, usually the greatest threat to the defense is one hot shooter. The best adjustment that you can make is to assign your best guard or forward to this player. Usually the other team will be setting screens to get its best offensive player open for a shot. If that is working, review the proper defense against the screen at halftime, using the players on the court to illustrate if necessary.

I try not to give too many instructions at halftime but rather to make basic offensive or defensive adjustments. For example, on offense often a guard will be moving the ball only to the right and forget to use the left side of the court. The defense quickly picks this up. The team often forgets to keep good spacing, and all the players contract into a small area. This ties up the offense because each time a player gets the ball there are at least two defenders around the player; so proper spacing usually needs to be emphasized to spread out the defense.

I almost never read the riot act to players at halftime. The one exception is when I feel they are not hustling. Two or three times a year we seem to have games where they are collectively lethargic and not moving. I save my read-the-riot-act speech for those occasions.

Likewise, building players into an emotional frenzy isn't my style. I feel that they are keyed up through their own nervous energy and don't need to be any higher before or during the game. On the contrary, usually they need to be calmed down, particularly in the middle of a close game.

REFEREES

At the beginning levels of basketball you get some beginning referees, and you get plenty of bad calls. One way to handle it is to whine and complain. I've tried that many times, and it feels pretty good, at least for a while; you can stomp around; you can be indignant, exasperated, dismayed; you can yell at a grown person who won't yell back. In the end, though, it sets a terrible example for your players. How can a coach expect his immature players to conduct themselves like adults on the court while the coach himself acts like a two-year-old throwing a temper tantrum?

Another way is to explain to your players that referees are people who really enjoy sports and are out there doing their best, and a lot of them aren't that experienced. Sure, they blow calls, but I blow calls as a coach too. The refs don't scream that *I've* messed up.

With that in mind, it's a lot easier to approach a referee during a time-out or at halftime and say, "Look, it's getting too rough under the basket; you're not calling enough fouls"; or "The other team is holding my players and it's not getting called." Whatever the complaint is, address it directly to the ref rather than yelling at the ref in front of other people. Tell your team what you're doing so that they understand it's a better way to deal with problems. Your players see you in control of the situation, and it increases your natural authority.

ANALYZE THE FLOW OF THE GAME

During the game a coach has dozens of things to keep track of: Is each of your players guarding the designated offensive player? Does the sub you put in know whom to guard? Is each player in proper defensive position?

In reality, one person can't keep track of everything that is developing on the court; there is simply too much going on. I try to videotape several games each year. In reviewing a tape, I am consistently surprised by the number of things that I did not notice. For example, one player on my team might be playing very good defense and another very poor defense, and I will not have picked that up. The coach has a floor-level view of the game, and it is not easy to see the whole court from that position.

Here is how I try to view the game:

▶ Most fans tend to watch the basketball. This gives you a view of only a few players on the court, at most. I try to keep looking away from the ball, particularly just after the game begins and just after each break in play, such as at the end of a quarter or after a time-out.
▶ At the beginning of the game and frequently during the game, I check to be sure that each defender is guarding an offensive player, that each defender is in the correct defensive position, and that we are getting weak-side help in our ball-pressure defense.
▶ After checking our defense, I look at our opponent's offense. What patterns are developing in their offense? How is our defense meeting their offensive strength?

▶ Which defense is the other team using? If it is a zone defense, are we using the proper offense to attack a zone, or are we playing into their defensive strengths?

▶ Each time we use a different offense, and especially at the beginning of the game, I want to be sure that players are in the right position and are doing what they are supposed to be doing on the court.

▶ I frequently check to see if the players are moving up and down the court quickly in our transition game. Players who are too slow in moving from one end of the court to the other are likely to need a breather for a few minutes.

▶ Your opponent is likely to change offense or defense during the course of the game; you need to be alert to these changes.

▶ In looking at our overall defense and offense, I also run through a mental checklist to see if we are doing the essential tasks correctly. For example, is our spacing good on the offense, are we attacking both the left and the right sides, are we getting the ball underneath successfully? On defense, are we getting back quickly and setting up, forcing the ball toward the sideline, getting early help with good recovery, getting weak-side help?

Changing Strategy

If the game suddenly starts going badly, it usually means that your opponent has successfully changed strategy. Before calling time-out,

▶ Watch what your opponent is doing.

▶ Watch your team to see if you can find where the problem lies.

▶ As soon as you have figured out the necessary adjustment, call time-out.

▶ Give your team specific instructions as to the adjustment you want made; for example, against a pressing defense, there will be areas of the court open, and you can

instruct your players to move toward those areas.

During the course of the game, make specific adjustments on defense to meet the other team's offensive maneuvering. For example, alternate defenders on the other team's best player so there's always a fresh person guarding that player; or have the defense back off to be less aggressive around the perimeter and pack into the middle more if the other team is successfully getting the ball underneath.

After each time-out and when a new quarter begins, I like to give our offense a new look because I assume their coach has made some adjustments to our offensive strategies that had been successful. Then, a few minutes later, I have the team go back to what was successful before in the hopes of confusing the opposition's defense.

Keep Calm

Young, inexperienced players tend to get too excited, particularly in a close game. During each break in play, they need your calming influence.

When the team comes back to the bench, I almost invariably will first say something reassuring, such as, "Okay, you're doing a good job out there." If I feel the players are too tight I might say, "This is really fun; I love a close game."

Don't speak in urgent tones to the players. Keep your voice calm and slow in telling them what you want them to do.

Rest Your Starters

When players get overtired, they are no longer effective on the court. The way to prevent this is to rest players from time to time during the game.

That is easy to say, but it is hard to do. You will often notice that as soon as you take a starter out of the game, the offense or defense will suffer at least somewhat. In years when there isn't much difference between the ability of the starters and the subs, I tend to rest the starters far more; in years when there is a significant difference in ability, the starters get much less rest.

It is hard to set up any specific formula for resting players because it really depends upon the quality of the substitutes and the ebb and flow of the game. For example, if my team is doing particularly well, I do not want to interrupt the flow of the game by removing starters. On the other hand, if things are going particularly badly on offense or defense, I may want to rush in a defensive or offensive specialist who may be able to provide the element that the team is lacking.

I try to handle substitutions in this way:

▶ The players are not particularly tired right after the game begins or after halftime.
▶ A player needs at least two, and preferably three, minutes for a rest. When I must rest a key player, I try to combine the rest period with an approaching time-out; for example, I often take my point guard out with one or two minutes to play at the end of the first and third quarters.
▶ I divide the starters into backcourt and frontcourt players. If I am playing two guards, I don't want both of my starters to be out at the same time. I will replace guard 1 with guard 3 about six minutes into the game. Guard 1 will rest about two minutes and then come back into the game in place of guard 2. If I am using a fourth guard or a fifth guard, I will use that guard to replace guard 3, my first substitute.
▶ In the frontcourt, I try to keep two of the three starting forwards in the game at all times. For example, I will send forward 4 in to replace forward 1 at about the four-minute mark. Two minutes later I will send forward 1 in for forward 2. Two minutes after that I will send forward 2 in for forward 3. In that way you can set up either a four- or five-player rotation among your forwards throughout the game.

FOUL TROUBLE

Coaches often bench players who are in foul trouble to keep them from fouling out. For example, many coaches would bench a player with two fouls until the end of the first half, even if the second foul was committed in the fourth or fifth minute of the game. The reasoning behind this strategy is that the player is essential in the final stage of the game and must not foul out early.

I handle foul trouble much differently. I want to have each of my starters in the game for as many total minutes as possible. Taking a player out of the game for long periods of time due to foul trouble essentially creates the same effect as though the player had fouled out. I feel it gives the other team a significant advantage if my starters are seated on the bench rather than playing in the game.

I caution players who are in foul trouble and repeat that caution from time to time, telling them to be less aggressive, especially on defense.

And I have found that most of the time the starters do not foul out and are available to me in the last few minutes of the game as well as the earlier stages.

INJURIES AND LOSS OF ELIGIBILITY

During the course of the season, it is not unusual to lose one or more players through injury or ineligibility due to poor grades. In both of these cases the kids are usually devastated; they've been enjoying themselves, having a good season, and then suddenly they are unable to play.

It would be easy to ignore these players because they can no longer be productive. But they should be more important to you than the points they can score or the rebounds they can pull down. Encourage them to stay with the team as managers, scorekeepers, or in any other capacity that you can think of.

We had a player with a bad knee injury who was a relatively weak shooter. Even with the injury, she could do two things: dribble the ball in place and shoot. So the kids brought out a rack of balls for her to dribble and shoot; she didn't have to chase them down, and every once in a while someone would come over and refill it. No doubt the injury was still very frustrating to her, but she made the most out of the situation and improved her shooting. Also, she stayed with the team while she was injured instead of drifting away as some players tend to do when they are ineligible or injured.

19
COACHING JUNIOR HIGH AND RECREATIONAL LEAGUE TEAMS

Coaches below the high school level usually don't have the luxury of adequate practice time. This chapter is devoted to suggesting how you can make the most of your limited practice time by stripping the offensive and defensive aspects of the game to the bare necessities.

DEFENSE

I would devote the bulk of my practice time to developing a man-to-man defense. At this level it is hard to develop strong offensive skills, and the priority should be on keeping the other team away from your basket. Also, an aggressive defense will produce steals that will turn into fast-break scoring opportunities.

The essential concept to teach is staying between your man and the basket with your back to the basket. Two other aspects need emphasis: First, be sure that players don't stray too far from the basket; it is unlikely that any opponent will be able to shoot effectively from farther out than the foul line. Many offenses operate a long distance from the basket in the hope of drawing the defense out. The defense should stay back and not pick up their men until about 12 feet from the basket. Also, you should stress staying with your opponent, whether or not he has

the ball. The one-on-one drill described in Chapter 10 is worth emphasizing.

Two occasions where your opponents will have good opportunities to score also require emphasis: the fast break and the out-of-bounds play (also discussed in Chapter 10).

If practice time permits, teach your players the principle of weak-side help (Chapter 11); your defense and rebounding will be significantly strengthened by bringing more players into the paint. There really is no penalty if the players forget their weak-side help responsibilities as they will be in basic man-to-man defensive positions in any event.

OFFENSE

The easiest, most basic offense to install is the 1-2-2 "closed" offense. It is a safe formation because passes are not likely to be stolen for lay-ups by the defense. It offers good perimeter shots and chances to score off offensive rebounds. The quick ball reversals also offer opportunities for driving to the basket against a zone that is slow to react.

This offense is also suitable for a beginning team because it can be expanded to take advantage of the players' skills as they develop. For example, at first the wings may only be able to pass and shoot the ball, but as the season progresses they may be able to drive the ball to the basket as well. The offense is discussed in detail in Chapter 12.

The closed offense is effective against any zone that has a two-man defensive front, such as a 2-1-2 or a 2-3. In the event the defense that you face is a man-to-man or a 3-2 zone, the offense can be converted into a 1-2-2 "open" offense, also discussed in Chapter 12. In this formation players are spread out, which provides opportunities for passing into the pivot area for inside shots or driving past defenders to the basket. If you have a tall player who is potentially dominating, the open offense gives you the opportunity to allow him to work one-on-one on a defender by spreading the court.

With these two formations, your offense will be prepared to operate against any defensive alignment. To develop the skills necessary for these formations, start with footwork and passing drills; when you have completed them, the closed offense is essentially in place.

By being able to field a reasonable offense without taking too much time, you can devote any additional time to developing individual skills: guards can start on proper dribbling sequences while forwards learn the power moves to the basket. The guards need not learn moves under the basket and the frontline players need not spend much time on dribbling, as there is not sufficient time to accomplish all of these goals.

You're unlikely to have time to teach players to drive the ball to the basket, but that might be included later in the season.

REBOUNDING

Two elements of rebounding are far more important than any others: first, rebounding aggressively by starting to move toward the basket as the shot is being taken; and second, moving to the proper position around the basket. These skills are discussed in Chapter 6.

The individual skills of jumping, jumping with your arms extended, and protecting the ball when you come down are important, as are all of the individual skills, but they can either be taught later or not at all, depending on your time considerations.

SHOOTING

The mechanics of shooting medium- and long-distance shots are discussed in Chapter 5. Except for lay-ups, all of your players' shots should be considered medium- or long-distance shots. In other words, they need to be taught to shoot the ball from chest height with either one or two hands. Emphasize the importance of getting a lot of bend in the legs and using the upward spring to provide power (see Figure 20.1) rather than pushing the ball or twisting their hands to whip the ball toward the basket.

Youth basketball is a good time to learn not to rush your shots. Players should not be concerned with having an occasional shot blocked; they should be concerned with getting set before they shoot.

DRIBBLING

Your players may be able to improve their dribbling skills dramatically if they practice dribbling at home. Give each player a specific assignment to dribble the ball—for example, three days a week for one hundred dribbles with each hand without looking at the ball. They can start out doing this in place and later, as their skills improve, at a walking pace, then a jogging pace, and finally at a running pace. Players should not move to the next level of difficulty until you have checked out their progress in practice.

PASSING AND SCREENING

These skills should be taught as practice time allows. Even one short practice on the correct way to throw a pass can save a lot of stolen passes during the season.

TRANSITION

Transition can be worked on in your scrimmages by requiring players to move up and down the court quickly and by using the switch drill described in Chapter 13.

20
PARENTS AND CHILDREN

I assume that you would like your child to play basketball well and enjoy doing so. How you introduce basketball to your child will have a major influence on whether that happens.

Here are two parents, each introducing an eight-year-old child to basketball; both parents have bought some equipment and are ready to get started:

The first parent is deadly serious. He or she repeatedly points out the child's mistakes and spends the entire time correcting the child's errors.

The basket is set at a regulation ten feet off the ground. The child is trying to reach a basket that is too high with a ball that is too heavy and too large to control. He almost never makes a shot.

The child keeps trying to do silly things, like throwing the ball over his head, but the parent discourages anything but practice.

The second child is at play on the basketball court. If he wants to do something silly, the parent has no objection and, in fact, joins in the play.

The child has a hoop set at eight feet, a level he can reach. The ball is small enough and light enough to control; he makes shots some of the time.

The parent, who is right-handed, is using his left hand to try to learn the same drib-bling skills that the child is learning. The parent spends a relatively short time teaching and a great deal of time playing with the child.

As you have no doubt guessed, I believe it is far more likely that the second child will have a positive experience learning to play basketball. He will be more likely to suggest to his parent that they go out and play basketball; or, if his parent suggests it, he will be enthusiastic about saying yes. Why not? He has a good time playing with his parent and is learning basketball in the process.

The first child initially may learn more basketball than the second child, as he is spending more time practicing. But he is not likely to have much enthusiasm for what he is doing or sustain an interest in basketball. In time, he is more likely to refuse to play basketball, and arguments between him and his parent will ensue.

It helps to take a long-term view of your objective. There is no need for children to learn basketball skills in a hurry; that is usually difficult in any event because they have short attention spans. It is more important that they have a positive experience with the sport and learn at a comfortable rate.

The coaching techniques discussed in Chapters 1 and 2 are even more applicable to younger students. They love to hear praise, especially from their father or mother.

Now that you are relaxed, ready to enjoy playing with your children while they learn, and ready to praise their efforts, let's look at the equipment you will need.

The only item of equipment that is absolutely necessary is a ball. Buy a ball that is smaller than a regular-size basketball. Any ball that has a true bounce and is the right size is better than a basketball that is too large and heavy. At least five different mini-basketball sizes are available. Korney Board Aids (Box 264, Roxton, Texas 75477-0264) publishes a catalog that lists minibasketballs by size and matches them to age and grade level. To order a catalog, call (800) 842-7772.

If you can put up a rim, that's fine, but almost anything will do—a carton, a waste-paper basket, etc. Put the basket at a height that your son or daughter can reach comfortably when shooting the ball. Your child won't learn bad habits shooting at a basket that is too low; he or she will surely learn bad habits shooting at a basket that is too high.

When the ball is too large, too heavy, or the basket is too high, children will adapt by pushing the ball at the basket rather than shooting it because they will need all their strength just to get the ball to the basket. Pushing is probably the worst shooting habit that anyone can acquire. Children also twist their hands, imparting a whiplike action to the ball, in order to put greater power into the shot; this, too, is likely to become a long-term habit that can significantly hinder their efforts to become good shooters.

For most kids in fourth, fifth, or sixth grade, a basket seven or eight feet high would be appropriate; an eight- or nine-foot basket would be right for most kids in junior high school.

Don't worry about fine points of the game. If you are teaching dribbling to someone who is seven years old, it really isn't important that the child first learn to dribble without looking at the ball or to dribble it off the fingertips. Instead, make the lesson into a game. Bring a watch and see if your child can dribble the ball for 30 seconds, or 15 or 20 bounces, without losing control. These goals can gradually be increased as the child's skills increase. If you are trying to teach passing, put up a tire or some other fixed object and have your child pass the ball through the opening in the tire.

Don't ask children to do work that their stage of development will not permit. For example, your child may be able to dribble or shoot the ball but may not be able to catch the ball. Trying to teach rebounding to someone who does not have the coordination to catch the ball when it is falling will only lead to frustration, disappointment, and a crunched finger or two.

Different children vary widely in their coordination, but there are certain guidelines that can be followed in determining what can be taught to children of different age levels: most kids can bounce a ball at an early age, perhaps four to seven, and shoot it with two hands; as they reach eight or nine, they are better able to catch the ball; by age ten they are able to learn most skills.

When children are old enough to learn the skill, follow the teaching sequences laid out in the earlier portions of the book for dribbling, passing, shooting, and rebounding. Just remember not to push too hard.

Most kids want to play "a real game." If they're able to dribble the ball and shoot it, you can adapt the rules of basketball to suit the occasion. Playing one-on-one is "just playing" for children but is a valuable form of practice: they are learning to play basically sound basketball in an unpressured environment.

If you're playing one-on-one with your child, here are some rules you may find useful:

▶ Don't block your child's shots. They really don't need to learn how to avoid having their shots blocked until they are well past the beginner's stage.

- Play with your opposite hand—you may find the game more interesting yourself.
- Don't run up a huge score; it only discourages a child.
- Don't call rules infractions, such as walking, until your child is no longer a beginner.
- Don't give long explanations about the rules or about how to perform different skills.

In order to play, your child will have to learn a little bit about defense. Start with the idea of staying between you and the basket and keeping his back to the basket (Chapter 10). Have your child dribble the ball and show him what it means to be between him and the basket; then let him try to stay between you and the basket as you dribble the ball.

Once your child is able to play a bit of defense, playing one-on-one games should work out very well—your child will be getting good practice in the most important element of man-to-man defense. At a later time, you can work in proper body position and footwork along the same sequential lines that are laid out in Chapter 10.

Regarding offensive skills,

- Have your child learn to dribble both "righty" and "lefty" as early as possible; after he learns to control the ball somewhat, have him dribble the ball without looking at it and follow the dribbling sequence laid out in Chapter 8.
- Teach your child to shoot from chest height with two hands, using the spring in his legs for strength. Note that the child shooting in Figure 20.1 has his rear end back and down and his legs in a crouched position. The shot is powered by springing upward out of the crouch. This leaves the arms and hands free to shoot the ball with proper mechanics. The correct manner of holding the ball and following through on the shot are discussed in Chapter 5. Once

Figure 20.1. A younger player gets extra strength by bending his legs and springing upward (not forward) when he shoots.

your child has learned to shoot the ball with proper mechanics, he will make his shots more frequently and find the game more enjoyable. As he becomes more proficient, use the shooting sequence laid out in Chapter 5.
- Make rebounding into a game; it is, after all, basically a race to the ball. If your child simply learns to go after rebounds, that is more than enough to start enjoying one-on-one or two-on-two basketball. Follow the sequence laid out in Chapter 6 as he becomes more adept at the game.
- Passing isn't important until you play two-on-two basketball. Don't worry about passing the ball until your child is able to catch it consistently. At that point, introduce passing along the lines set out in Chapter 7.
- Footwork becomes important around fifth or sixth grade when your child starts to

play in rec leagues or on school teams. Follow the sequence laid out in Chapter 4.

▶ Have your child face the basket on offense. From that position he can shoot or drive. The tendency of most children is to put their backs to the basket, which makes it difficult to shoot, pass, or drive. It is a completely unproductive way of attacking the hoop.

Basketball is fun to play; it is a game and not a chore. If you treat it as a game and don't push your child too hard, he will most likely learn to really enjoy basketball and want to play it. The rest is easy.

21
CONCLUSION

At the start of each season, when our scrimmages are really ragged, I picture John Wooden sitting in the deserted stands, shaking his head, trying to decide whether he is seeing basketball or jungleball. At that point it seems an almost impossible undertaking to get the team ready to play. In addition to all the individual skills to be learned, there are the small matters of the defense, the offense, and the press break.

A few weeks go by, and we start to look like a basketball team. Now, before the first game, I begin overestimating my players. The offense seems to work well when there are no defenders on the court; the defense seems almost impenetrable, especially when the substitutes try to score against the starters.

As the season gets underway, reality sets in as strengths and weaknesses become more apparent under game conditions. Sooner or later there is a low point when the opponent has a lead and you feel helpless to stem the tide. You call time-outs, change the offense, adjust the defense, try a full-court press, but nothing seems to work, and the team loses.

These losses are always hard to take, but I find solace in the words of tennis professional Vic Braden. Braden had a ten-part TV series on tennis technique and strategy. During one segment he read a letter from a viewer who had this problem: when he stayed

in the backcourt, his opponent was beating him because the opponent had better strokes from the backcourt; so he followed Braden's advice and charged the net. Now he found that his opponent had better passing shots and a good overspin lob.

The viewer's question was, "What should I do now?" Braden's answer was, "Lose. This guy is much better than you are."

As a coach, you can only do so much to affect the outcome of the game. When you encounter a better team that is well coached, you are likely to lose. Losing is part of coaching; so too are injuries, ineligibility, and the many other difficulties that arise during the season.

These setbacks have a positive side for your players: experiencing losses and difficulties is part of growing up; as players go through the hard times, with the support of their teammates, they grow in maturity. That growth is part of the educational purpose of school sports.

Winning is an exhilarating experience for the players and the coach. Several years ago, our team made the finals of a 16-team tournament. The kids were exhausted: playing three hard-fought games in two days plus attending school and dealing with the long commute to the tournament each day had taken their toll.

Frankly, our opponents looked scary. They

were tall, athletic, well drilled, and they were the defending champions. We played nervously throughout the first quarter and were losing 12–3.

In the second quarter, our defense started to assert itself, enabling us to draw within five points at halftime. The other team now looked as weary as we were; more important, our players realized that they could compete evenly against their opponents.

We drew even after three quarters. Our gas tank was empty, but the team was running on sheer determination; the girls were diving for loose balls and contesting every rebound. When one of the starters needed a rest, or fouled out, a sub would replace her and get the job done.

The teams battled evenly throughout the fourth quarter; both teams raised their level of play. We were one point ahead and had possession of the ball with one minute to play. One of their players crashed into our ball handler, who crumpled to the ground. She scraped herself off the ground, shook off the wooziness, and made the foul shots that provided the ultimate margin of victory.

We went nuts—players, parents, and coach. Our team had overcome injury, exhaustion, and self-doubt to win the tournament. We collected a bunch of trophies, including the MVP award for the player who made those last foul shots.

We all need our victories, our moments to excel. Outside of sports, there are few opportunities to have an experience like that one.

Less dramatic, little magical moments occur in practice and in games from time to time. In one game, Angie, our point guard, drove past her defender and headed for the hoop. The opposing center was guarding Melanie, our center. Their center moved over to block Angie's path to the basket, leaving Melanie unguarded.

As Melanie moved into scoring position, Angie feathered a bounce pass to her. Melanie scooped it up, turned, and made the shot. As the girls ran downcourt, Mel pointed a finger at Angie, acknowledging Angie's pass.

It only took a few seconds, but there it was: perfect execution, communication, and cooperation. And not a word was spoken. It was basketball at its best.

Apart from the highs and lows of winning and losing, participating in a basketball program offers ample rewards to players and coaches. The players feel the satisfaction of giving their best effort and of mastering various skills. They learn to rely on themselves; they learn that the world doesn't end with losing or winning; they learn the importance of teamwork; and they learn the importance of supporting and being supported by the teammates on and off the court.

The coach is rewarded in two ways. He or she can take pride in the individual improvement of the players and in bringing order out of chaos, in molding a group of players into a cohesive team. Perhaps more important, the coach experiences the satisfaction of seeing his players grow in maturity and self-confidence through their positive experiences in his program.

A year after she made those foul shots in the tournament final, that player told me she would remember the feeling she had at that moment for the rest of her life. Another player wrote an epic poem about the tournament.

With rewards like these, and terrific kids to work with, coaching basketball is the place to be.

INDEX

Aggressiveness, 37–38, 92
  drills, 38
Arm position
  rebounding, 40
Athletic skills
  and tryouts, 127, 129

Backboard, 29, 33
Backspin, 28, 29, 45, 49
Bad habits, 23–24, 150
Balance, 18
  and shooting, 24
Ball fake, 51, 73
Ball position
  and shooting, 28–29
Ball-pressure defense, 87–95
  advantages, 87
  channeling ball to sidelines, 87–88
  drills, 92–95
  help-side positioning, 89–91, 94
  on the line, up the line, 88–89, 94
Baseball pass, 49–50, 117
  releasing, 50
  throwing, 50
Baseline jump shot, 29
Basketball skills
  and tryouts, 127, 129–30
Basketball's Zone Presses: A Complete Coaching
  Guide (Paye), 125
Bennett, Dick, 95
Blocking out, 41–42

Body position
  chest pass, 45
  defense, 76
  dribbling, 55–56
  screens, 51–52
  and shooting, 24–26
Bounce pass, 48–49
Box formation, 116–17
Braden, Vic, 153
Breakaway lay-up, 33
Breathing, 31

Calmness, 141, 142
Catch and dribble, 60
Changing hands, 58
Chart, tryout, 128–29
Chest pass, 45–47
Choosing players
  for defense, 123–24
  for the squad, 130
Closed formation, 98–100
Coaching, 1–2. *See also specific issues*
  communication, 11–12
  dealing with unacceptable behavior, 11
  game-day, 139–44
  giving directions, 9–10
  junior high, 145–47
  limiting what is taught, 10
  objectives, 3–5
  recreational teams, 145–47
  sequence, 13–14
  techniques, 7–12

Collapse to the offensive player, 92
Communication, 11–12, 79, 92, 134
    defense, 79, 92
Concentration, 28, 47
Conditioning
    drills, 136–37
Cone drill, 58–59
Coordination, 150
Crosscourt pass, 50–51
Crossover dribbling, 56–57
Cutting, 21–22, 66

Dead-front position, 91–92, 94
Defense, 2, 12, 75–86, 97–105, 145. *See also specific
        defenses*
    adjustments, 124–25
    against an out-of-bounds play, 82–83
    against the fast break, 79–82
    ball away from sidelines, 113
    ball-pressure, 87–95
    body position, 76
    choosing players, 123–24
    communication, 79, 92
    distance from offensive player, 77
    drills, 77, 78–79, 82
    footwork, 76–77
    guarding post player, 83
    pivot-area, 91–92
    practice, 135
    pressing, 53, 55, 113–25
    protecting the basket, 75
    rebounding, 41–42
    screens, 82, 85, 92
    spreading out, 113–14
Directions
    clear, 10
    simple, 9–10
    and tryouts, 127
"Dog fight," 38
"Dribble War," 58
Dribbling, 55–61, 129, 146
    body position, 55–56
    crossover, 56–57
    drills, 57–59
    hand position, 56
    practice, 135
Drills, 2. *See also specific drills*
    aggressiveness, 38
    all-purpose, 53
    ball-pressure defense, 92–95

breaking the press, 53
conditioning, 136–37
defense, 77, 78–79, 82
dribbling, 57–59
driving, 2, 20–21
fakes, 51
fast break, 110–11
first, 132
follow-up, 132
footwork, 2
gapping, 123
inbounding ball, 53
jump stop, 22, 53
jumping, 40–41
lay-up, 33
moving to basket as shot is taken, 38–39
moving to get open, 53
offense, 105
passing, 2, 17–18, 47
pivoting, 53
protecting the ball, 53
rebounding, 39–40
retreat, 125
screens, 53
selection, 132–33
shooting, 19
transition, 109–11
trapping, 121–22
Driving
    ball to left, 64
    to the basket, 63–64
    drills, 2, 20–21
    footwork, 19–20
Drop step, 68–70

Elbow position
    chest pass, 45
    and rebounding, 41–42
    and shooting, 25, 26
Eligibility, 143–44
Extra step, 72–73
Eye fake, 51
Eye-hand coordination, 129

Fakes, 51, 66
Fast break
    defense, 79–82
    drills, 110–11
    footwork, 110–11
    three-on-two, 81

transition, 109–10
two-on-one, 80
two-on-two, 81
Fast-break
practice, 136
Fast-passing drill, 47
Fingers
and shooting, 26, 27
Five-on-five scrimmage, 130
Follow-through, 28
Following directions. *See also* Directions
and tryouts, 127
Footwork
baseball pass, 49
defense, 76-77
drills, 2
driving, 19–20
fast break, 110–11
offense, 15–22, 67
passing, 16–17
practice, 135, 151
shooting, 18–19
Forearm position, 25
Forwards
positioning, 101
up formation, 104
Foul shots, 31, 43–44
Frontline player, 108
Full-court press, 119. *See also* Pressing defense
practice, 136

Game day, 139–44
Game flow, 141–42
Game plan, 139. *See also* Strategy
Game time, 140–41
Gapping, 122–23
drills, 123
Give and go, 103, 105
Guard and wings, 136
Guarding, 108. *See also* Defense; Man-to-man
defense
match-up, 140
substitutions, 140
Guards
fast break, 110

Half-court defense, 119
Halftime, 140–41
Hand position
dribbling, 56

and lay-ups, 34
passing, 46
and shooting, 27–28
Hands, changing, 58
Head fake, 51, 73
Help-side, 83–85
positioning, 89–91
High-arc shot, 29
High post, 102–3

I formation, 116
Inbounding ball
drills, 53
Inbounds pass, 107, 116, 119–20
Injuries, 143–44

Jack-in-the-box offense, 104–5
Jogging, 58
Jump shot, 28, 30, 69, 71
baseline, 29
elbow position, 25
Jump stop, 22, 69, 70, 70–71
drills, 53
Jumping drills, 40–41
Junior high teams, 145–47
Junior varsity, 3

Knight, Bobby, 7–8, 12
Korney Board Aids, 150
Krzyzewski, Mike, 7–8, 12

Lay-up, 71
drill, 33, 58
underhand, 73
Leverage, 32
Lob pass, 92
Long-distance shots, 31–32
Loose balls, 37
Losing, 153

Man-to-man defense, 75–77, 84–85, 101–3, 113–16,
145, 151
Medium shots, 31–32
Moving to get open
drills, 53
Muscle memory, 14

No-walk drill, 21
Nondominant hand, 57

Offense, 2, 145–46
   beginning level, 97
   categorizing, 84
   closed formation, 98–100
   drills, 105
   footwork, 15–22
   give and go, 103, 105
   high post, 102–3
   jack-in-the-box, 104–5
   1-2-2 offense, 98
   open formation, 100–102
   passing, 47–48
   practice, 135
   rebounding, 42–43
   shooting, 65–67
   up formation, 103–4
One-on-one drill, 78
One-pass position, 90
1-2-2 offense, 98, 145
   outer triangle, 98
Open formation, 100–102
Out-of-bounds play
   defense, 82–83
Overhand shot, 33
Overspin, 28, 49

Parents, 149–52
Pass-and-cut-away drill, 17
Pass-and-screen-away drill, 18
Pass fake, 63–64
Pass from the perimeter, 47
Passing, 1, 45–51, 129, 147, 151
   baseball pass, 49–50, 117
   bounce pass, 48–49
   chest pass, 45–47
   crosscourt pass, 50–51
   diagonal, 124
   drills, 2, 17–18, 47
   footwork, 16–17
   hand position, 46
   inbounds, 107, 116, 119–20
   risky, 113
   shooting and driving drill, 20–21
   sidelines, 124
Passing and shooting drill, 19
Passive defense, 105
Paye, Burrall, 125
Perimeter player, 101
   triple-threat position, 66

Pivot-area defense, 91–92
Pivoting, 16, 71–72
   baseball pass, 49
   bounce pass, 48–49
   drills, 53
   driving, 20
   drop step, 68
   either foot, 67
   left foot for, 15, 67
   right foot for, 60
   shot fake, 63
Players
   backcourt vs. frontcourt, 130, 143
   for defense, 123–24
   frontline, 108
   number on team, 127
   perimeter, 66, 101
   post, 83
   for squad, 130
   starters, 142–43
   types, 127–28
Player's perspective, 10–11
Playing time, 134
Positive experience, 3–4, 149–50, 154
"Possessed," 58
Post player
   guarding, 83
Post position, 49, 66, 101
   high post, 102
Power ball to basket, 71–72
Power move, 64–65
Practice, 131–37. *See also* Drills
   defense, 135
   division of time, 132
   dribbling, 135
   fast-break, 136
   footwork, 135
   full-court press, 136
   offense, 135
   schedule, 134–36
   scrimmage, 135
   sequence, 135
   shooting, 135
Pressing defense, 55
   adjustments, 124–25
   breaking the press, 113–17
      drills, 53
   transition, 125
Pressure Defense—A System (Bennett), 95

Priorities, 2, 131–37
Protecting the ball
  drills, 53
Pushing the ball, 150

Quick inbounds pass, 116

Rebounding, 37–44, 146, 151
  arm position, 40
  defensive, 39, 41–42
  drills, 39–40, 94
  moving to basket as shot is taken, 38–39
  offensive, 42–43
  position, 39, 80, 91, 100
  transition, 108
Recreational teams, 145–47
"Red light–green light," 110
Referees, 141
Relay race, 58
Rescheduling, 11
Rest, 142–43
Retreat drills, 125
Reward vs. punishment, 7–9
Roster, 131
Rules, 4
Running, 129
Running lay-up, 33–35

Schedule for practice, 131, 134–36
Scramble, 38
Screens, 1, 51–53, 102, 147
  body position, 51–52
  defense, 82, 85, 92
  drills, 53, 94
  setting, 52, 116
Scrimmage, 14, 44, 75, 132
  practice, 135
Sequence, 13–14
  practice, 135
Shallow-triangle position, 90–91, 93
Shell drill, 78–79, 92–93
Shooting, 23–35, 30, 130, 146
  bad habits, 23–24, 150
  balanced position, 24
  ball position, 28–29
  baseline jump shot, 29
  body position, 24–26
  drills, 19
  footwork, 18–19

hand position, 27–28
high-arc shot, 29
leverage, 32
long-distance shots, 31–32
mechanics, 30
medium shots, 31–32
from outside, 64
positions, 19, 65–67
practice, 135
repetitions, 30
routine, 31
seam parallel to floor, 24
shorter-distance shots, 29–30
shoulder forward, 23
timing, 66–67
two-handed set shot, 32
Shooting and driving drill, 20
Shooting drills, 2
Shooting range, 26, 32, 77
Shorter-distance shots, 29–30
Shot chart, 64
Shot fake, 51, 63
Shoulder position
  shooting, 23
Sidelines pass, 124
Sidespin, 23, 24
Skills, 1, 2. *See also specific skills*
  learning new, 14
  limiting what is taught, 10
  shooting, 2
Slide-down move, 70–71
Speed
  transition, 107
Spin move, 67–68
Strategy, 139, 142
Stride forward, 16–17
Substitutes, 133–34, 140
"Switch," 112

Teaching methods, 2, 9–12. *See also* Coaching
  giving directions, 9–10
  limiting what is taught, 10
Team spirit, 4, 131, 133
3-1-1 press, 119–20
Three-guard formation, 114
Three-man continuous drill, 136–37
Three-man weave, 136
Three-on-three game, 130
Three-point shot, 32

Three-second violation, 81
Time-out, 140
Timing
    shooting, 66–67
    up formation, 104
Transition, 147
    after a basket, 107–8
    after rebound, 108–9
    from defense to offense, 107–11
    drills, 109–11
    fast break, 109–10
    game, 112
    from offense to defense, 111–12
    pressing defense, 125
    speed, 107
Trapping, 113–14, 120–22
    drills, 121–22
Triangle drill, 47
Triple-threat position, 15–16, 18–20
    driving, 63
    and passing, 47
    perimeter player, 66
    up formation, 104
Tryout chart, 128–29

Tryouts, 127–30
    and athletic skills, 127, 129
    and basketball skills, 127, 129–30
    and following directions, 127, 129
Two-on-two rebounding drill, 39

Underhand lay-up, 34
Underhand shot, 33
Up formation, 103–4
    forwards, 104
    timing, 104

Vertical jump, 129
Video, 95

Walking violations, 22
Warm up, 132, 135
Winning, 3–4, 153
Wooden, John, 153
Wrist
    limp, 28
    and shooting, 23, 25, 26, 33

Zigzag drill, 59, 78–79
Zone defense, 75, 100, 113, 115